UNFORGOTTEN
VOICES FROM HEART MOUNTAIN

by Joanne Oppenheim and Nancy Matsumoto

To those who shared their voices—may they never be forgotten.

CONTENTS

INTRODUCTION

Voices from Heart Mountain and a Note About Our Own Voices

In downtown Los Angeles, only a few small shops in Little Tokyo were open along First Street on that Sunday afternoon of December 7, 1941. As news of the Japanese early dawn attack on Pearl Harbor reached the mainland, Americans all over the country sat close to their radios. Perhaps the most anxious among them were those of Japanese descent who lived along the West Coast of the United States.

Almost at once, in the cities and towns where they lived, a campaign of hate and suspicion spread. Newspapers and radio commentators whipped up fears that those of Japanese ancestry were not to be trusted. Vitriolic anti-Japanese hatred existed before the war, but now the long simmering broth of racism boiled up into hysteria that soon led to the incarceration of all those of Japanese descent living on the West Coast. It made no difference that two-thirds of them were American citizens.

Historians have written scholarly books about this shameful chapter in our history. This book is a companion tome, a collection of stories told by those who lived as prisoners inside of an American concentration camp, as well as those who worked as administrators and teachers inside the camp and some who lived in the near-by towns of Cody and Powell. Many voices in this collection come from diaries, letters, and newspapers written as the events they describe were happening. Others are from interviews recorded decades later, tempered by time and memory. They are the voices of people from both sides of the barbed wire fence in a place known as Wyoming's Heart Mountain Relocation Center.

Some of these stories are from Nancy Matsumoto's own family.

Nancy:

All four of my grandparents, along with my parents and their siblings were among those imprisoned. They lived in Los Angeles and Santa Monica, grocery store owners on my mother's side, and a jack-of-all trades on my father's side. My grandfather worked as a butler for Buster Keaton, a gardener, itinerant fruit picker, and Ocean Park Pier concession stand owner.

On my mother's side of the family, three generations lived under one roof, and all were imprisoned. My maternal grandparents were 41 and 52 when Pearl Harbor was bombed, living with my great-grandmother and three children. My mother, her older sister, and her brother were

9, 16 and 18, respectively. My uncle was a sophomore at UCLA. The family was given days to sell their business and pack only what they could carry. Under the guard of shotgun and bayonet-wielding soldiers they were taken first to a re-purposed horse-racing track and then to a desolate prison camp in Heart Mountain, Wyoming.

My father was 13 at the time. His family was taken to the Manzanar prison camp in the high desert of California. Like most Sansei, or third-generation Japanese Americans, I didn't know much about this chapter of my family's life until I was probably in high school. Even then, I had only a hazy notion of what had happened to them. No one talked about it, there was too much repressed shame and anger, I later realized. Like many of my generation, I never did learn much about those years from her family—a terrible loss of family lore. I know that period shaped them, and me, in profound ways that I'm still trying to understand.

In fact, that is how this book came to be.

Joanne:

My own interest in the incarceration began while searching for a Japanese American classmate, who never spoke of her imprisonment during World War II. My search led me to the Japanese American National Museum, where I not only found my classmate, but the stories of Dear Miss Breed and the diary of Stanley Hayami. Both gems of JANM's archives became the center of my research and writing for most of a decade. As an American, I needed to know how my country could have done this to its own people. What had happened to the Nikkei certainly resonated with my own Jewish family's history of the death camps of Eastern Europe.

Nancy's interest in her family's own missing stories led her to a talk I gave at NYU in 2008 about my book, Stanley Hayami: Nisei Son. In fact, by the time we met, I had been shaping what I called, my "Voices" book for several years. In 2004, I started collecting first-hand accounts from those who were imprisoned at Heart Mountain, many of them, former boy scouts. I thought then of doing a book for young people. By 2005, the story kept growing with stories about the draft and the resisters. After traveling to California, Wyoming, Washington, D.C., and even to a HM reunion in Las Vegas, I had assembled an authentic history of the incarceration, one told in the very human words of those who were there. Yet, there was something incomplete about the manuscript. So, it sat in a drawer, a manuscript-in-waiting, for most of another decade.

Over the years, Nancy became a friend. She read the "Voices" manuscript and we talked about how it might best be presented, in a book, a film, a play? More than once, I mentioned that what was missing was the voice of someone like Nancy—and the experience of being heir to that history. Nancy's Sansei voice, representing a Japanese American family whose first and second generations had all been imprisoned became the through line that could tie all the stories together.

So, we began collaborating.

These are stories that should never have happened. Many were told as cautionary tales, hoping to prevent history from repeating itself. Yet it has. While we were working, the crisis at our Southern border began as thousands of foreign-born children and adults, Latino refugees from Central and South America, were being held in American detention centers. They came to America seeking protection, with the desire to live in peace, as millions of immigrants have done in the past. Their stories eerily echo our past. More recently, hate groups, white supremacists have ushered in a new era of Jim Crow style violence directed at Black and Brown people. A new surge of anti-Asian hate has swept the country and the numbers of antisemitic attacks have become reminiscent of Nazi Germany in the 1930s. Racism, religious bigotry, and anti-immigrant sentiments are as current today as they were in 1942—only the targets of the attacks have broadened.

These Unforgotten Voices from Heart Mountain should remind us of what happens when the foundational principles of our democracy are forgotten, and we fail to protect the civil liberties of others. Unless we defend the rights of all there is no telling, who will be next.

First they came for the socialists, and I did not speak out—Because I was not a socialist.
Then they came for the trade unionists, and I did not speak out—Because I was not a trade unionist.
Then they came for the Jews, and I did not speak out—Because I was not a Jew.
Then they came for me — and there was no one left to speak for me.

-MARTIN NIEMOLLER (1892–1984), GERMAN LUTHERAN PASTOR

Joanne Oppenheim and Nancy Matsumoto
New York City and Toronto, 2023

READER'S GUIDE

Abbreviations to Know:

FPC – Fair Play Committee	NARA – National Archives and Records Administration
HMS – Heart Mountain Sentinel	MM – Mike Mackey Collection, Washington State University
JANM – Japanese American National Museum	WRA – War Relocation Authority
JFO – Joanne F. Oppenheim	WWII – World War 2

Key Words to Know:

Issei first generation Japanese who immigrated to the United States; Issei were not permitted to become U.S. citizens, they were forced by law to remain "involuntary aliens" until 1952, long after WWII. **Nisei** second generation, children of the Issei; Japanese Americans born in the United States and therefore, citizens. **Sansei** third-generation Japanese Americans, children of the Nisei. **Yonsei** fourth-generation Japanese Americans. **Nikkei** refers to all people of Japanese origin in the United States.

In reprinting diary entries and letters we have kept the original misspellings and grammatical errors; keeping them authentic as the "Voices" throughout.

Testimony: You will find entries marked as testimony throughout the book. These are but a small sampling of the unforgettable testimony given by 750 witnesses who testified during the 1981 hearings of the Congressionally established Commission on Wartime Relocation and Internment of Civilians (CWRIC), whose mandate was to investigate the policies directed at Japanese Americans during World War II.

About the camps: Santa Anita was just one of 16 temporary Assembly Camps used from March to October 1942, where the Nikkei were held until being moved further inland. They were racetracks and fairgrounds and under the control of the U.S. Army. Heart Mountain was just one of ten Relocation Camps controlled by the War Relocation Authority. There were six U.S. Department of Justice camps that were used to house so-called "dangerous persons" of Japanese ancestry.

About racist language and images: Some of the language and images contained in this book in letters, documents, and interviews are highly offensive and racist. We have elected to publish them uncensored to illustrate the thinking of the time and do not in any way condone the views expressed.

AMERICA IS AT WAR!

Pearl Harbor by Stanley Hayami, Tempo 1944, Heart Mountain High Yearbook

NOB, JR. HIGH STUDENT

Nobuyuki Shimokochi, a 13-year-old from downtown Los Angeles, attended Lafayette Jr. High with many other Japanese Americans. A city kid, he helped out in his parents' store. His kid sister, three and a half years younger, was learning to play the piano.

It was about noon when I left church, jumped onto a streetcar, the 'U-car', placed 7 cents in the coin box and rode three or four miles down Central Avenue. The trolley came to a squealing stop when I pulled the buzzer cord at the 2300 block and walked a half a block to the "Sun Market", a little Mom and Pop grocery my parents operated. Our living quarters were in the back of the store.

I was eating a quick lunch when a neighbor came running in the front door shouting, 'Pearl Harbor was bombed!'

NOBUYUKI SHIMOKOCHI INTERVIEW WITH JFO 11/12/04

FRANK, COLLEGE AGE STUDENT

When his father became ill, Frank Emi left college to take care of the family business. It wasn't exactly his plan, but it was his duty to care for his father and his business.

I was at work in our produce market on 11th and Alvarado Street, counting the days 'til the New Year 1942. I was wondering if the baby we were expecting would be born before 1941 ended. I was studying to be a pharmacist at City College in L.A., but when my father got ill, I had to leave school to run the family business. Soon I'd be a father. Would I ever go back to school? For now, it seemed unlikely. I remember reaching up and flicking on the radio. At first, I figured what I was hearing was another of those War of the World shows... you know, that radio broadcast when everyone all over the country was terrified...when we all thought Martians had landed. Only, that day, when I turned the dial—other stations were announcing the same thing— 'Pearl Harbor is being attacked!'

I remember thinking—maybe we are at war.

FRANK EMI INTERVIEW WITH JFO 10/20/05

YOSH, COLLEGE AGE STUDENT

Yosh Kuromiya was just getting started as an art major at Pasadena Junior College. His family had a successful produce store in Monrovia that they had just enlarged.

That Sunday—my brother was getting engaged. They were announcing their engagement at a party that night, Dec. 7th— of all times. Early that day, we went to the used car lots in Pasadena. Since he would have his own family now, he needed a car...as we came onto this one car lot, a guy came storming out of his little mobile office and chased us out of there.

'We're not going to sell any cars to Japs!' he was yelling and we said to each other, 'What's eating him?'

So, we went back to the car and headed for the next lot. Meantime, we put the radio on and that's when we first got the announcement... about Pearl Harbor. Needless to say, we decided to go home after that and just forget about the car.

People stopped by and assured us that we're going to be O.K. 'Don't worry!' they said. And I was insulted that they would even suggest that there was anything wrong with us! It was pretty clear we were American citizens and it's really clear that WE were attacked—it just happened to be my parents' country that did it. It seems as though they expected us to apologize for being Japanese or apologize for the Japanese bombing Pearl Harbor.

Yosh Kuromiya interview with JFO 10/21/05

STANLEY, HIGH SCHOOL STUDENT

Stanley Hayami was an honor student at Mark Keppel High in Alhambra. His family had a nursery in San Gabriel. He had hopes of going to Berkeley like his older brother and sister. He liked writing and drawing and had started lots of diaries, but this is one he kept going for several years.

In the afternoon business slowed down to a standstill, not a customer came for about an hour, so I went back to the house and turned on the radio. The announcer kept butting in 'Attention to all men in service. Report at once to your station. All leaves cancelled' Then tuning in on a news broadcast I heard the stunning news. 'Pearl Harbor bombed!'

I turned off the radio and rushed out front and told Pa and Ma.

That night we all felt as if we were ... still having a nightmare. Obasan [Aunt] called and told about what was happening in L.A. Ojisan, my Uncle was taken away immediately...The FBI rounded up a lot of people that night...Dec. 7th. He was a big car dealer and he was influential in the community.

We all went to sleep that night wondering what was going to happen to us.

STANLEY HAYAMI DIARY, DECEMBER 7, 1942,
JANM

Two days later Stanley wrote to his sister at Berkeley...

Dear Sach,

Please come home as soon as you can. Everything is O.K. down here, except Pa's money has been frozen and there is hardly any business. I guess we will have a sad x'mas this year. We will have to save our money and not buy any presents. I hope the war will be over in a hurry!!

Stan

Like all Issei, first generation Japanese immigrants, the Hayamis could not own property. To get around the law, Japanese parents bought property in the name of their American born children.

REI, HIGH SCHOOL STUDENT

Reiko Ohara grew up in Little Tokyo in LA. Her father was a well-known businessman. Rei had just started high school. She loved going to the movies, playing the piano, and listening to the Hit Parade on the radio. She had two younger brothers.

That night the smell of smoke filled the yards of Little Tokyo. People started burning anything Japanese—scrolls, letters, photographs, books—afraid they'd be accused of being spies.

We were already in bed when we heard excitement at our front door. An FBI agent and two LA Police with shotguns in their hands came to take Father away! We had no idea why Father was arrested or that he was one of hundreds of Japanese aliens, on a list to be arrested in the event of war.

Our Father, was a leader of the Chamber of Commerce in Little Tokyo. He ran a business his own father started. He manufactured Japanese fish cakes—he was a very successful businessman. In fact, the whole family had just returned from a long visit to Grandmother, Mother's mother, our Sobo in Japan. That was part of the problem. Anyone who went to Japan in those days was treated like a spy.

The next day we went from one jailhouse to another, trying to find out where Father had been taken. We kids got to see him just once before he was sent to federal prison in Montana. He didn't return for another two and a half years!

REIKO OHARA KASAMA & TOSH OHARA INTERVIEW WITH JFO 11/04/04

The next morning, up and down the west coast, newsboys shouted everyone's worse fears. The enemy would attack the mainland. Just two days later the headlines read:

JAPAN PLANES NEAR S.F.
4 RAID ALARMS
San Francisco Chronicle, December 9, 1941

ENEMY PLANES SIGHTED OVER CALIFORNIA COAST
Los Angeles Times, Dec. 9, 1941

But, the headlines were untrue. There were, in fact, no Japanese planes near San Francisco, although air raid sirens went off and people panicked in Los Angeles and San Francisco. Everyone was sure that bombs were about to fall. Those suspected enemy planes turned out to be weather balloons that our anti-aircraft guns fired at.

West Coast Jitters continued. First Lady Eleanor Roosevelt traveled to California with New York City's Mayor Fiorello La Guardia, as co-chairs of Civil Defense. The First Lady talked with women, urging them to lay in supplies of food and first aid equipment and to choose a safe room away from windows. In other words, it was not a question of if an attack was coming —only a question of when. Indeed, on the night of February 24th, air raid sirens went off as the "Battle of Los Angeles" began. Reports of enemy aircraft, 'about 25 planes' lead to the menacing sound of anti-aircraft artillery erupting over LA. "Air Battles Rages Over Los Angeles" the Los Angeles Herald Examiner reported.

The LA Times told it like this...

> *Roaring out of a brilliant moonlit western sky, foreign aircraft flying both in large formation and singly flew over Southern California early today and drew heavy*

barrages of anti-aircraft fire – the first ever to sound over United States continental soil against an enemy invader.

It seems everyone had forgotten President Roosevelt's wise advice — "The only thing to fear is fear itself."

That night, the frightening barrage of anti-aircraft artillery that lit up the sky was real, but the enemy planes were not. They were what the Secretary of the Navy, Frank Knox, called "a false alarm...attributed to jittery nerves."

ALAN and PETER SIMPSON, CODY BOYS

Fifth and sixth graders, Alan and Peter Simpson, grew up in the little town of Cody in Wyoming. Both Simpson brothers were Boy Scouts and acolytes at the Episcopal Church.

It was a warm sort of day here in Cody. We were school kids, 10 and 11 years old, playing outside when a neighbor came running down the hill shouting, "We've been attacked at Pearl Harbor!" He was a young fellow with a reputation for telling tall tales. My mother thought it was just another story, but, just on a hunch, she decided to go inside and listened to the radio and sure enough that's exactly what had happened and we were locked on the radio all afternoon.

My memory is of going to church that night, right here in town. My mother, of course, reacted – we had relatives in the service. Dad had a nephew who was a Navy pilot and there was our cousin Harry.

That night in Cody, we had no idea that by summer the

government would build the third largest city in our state just a few miles away from our quiet homes, a city that would be a prison.

HON. ALAN K. SIMPSON, FORMER U.S. SENATOR, AND PETER K. SIMPSON INTERVIEW WITH JFO 8/27/04

No one knew yet that a Wyoming boy, James O. Morgareidge, a 21-year-old sailor from Deaver, died aboard the USS Arizona, one of five battleships lost that day. With 1,177 men aboard, the USS Arizona took more men to the bottom with her than any ship in recorded U.S. Naval history.

KAZ, ELEMENTARY SCHOOL STUDENT

Kaz Shiroyama grew up in a Japanese fishing community in Wilmington, not far from Los Angeles. His parents came to America by way of Mexico. His father was a fisherman, his mother worked in the cannery. He was a 6th grader at Avalon Boulevard Elementary School.

Kaz Shiroyama

I was coming home from school one day, I don't know how many days after Pearl Harbor, but there was this little black coupe parked in front of our home. In the car were two FBI agents with some man in the middle. It was just a two-door black coupe and I saw my mother standing outside on the porch there and she was crying. I was confused. I didn't know what was going on. She kind of shoved me over to the car—at the time I didn't realize my father was in the car and she said, 'Go say good-bye to Papa.'

Still, I didn't understand what was going on. I walked to the car and saw my father sandwiched between the two FBI agents and I reached over the agent sitting next to the window and shook my father's hand. And [Kaz took a long emotional pause before going on] we didn't see him for three years after that.

KAZ SHIROYAMA INTERVIEW WITH JFO 11/7/04

AMY, ELEMENTARY SCHOOL STUDENT

Amy Iwasaki Mass was just six-years old when the war began. Yet, the memories of those frightening days have never been forgotten. In 1981, during Congressional hearings held in 10 American cities, many of those who had been incarcerated finally gave words and face to a tragic story.

> *The FBI picked up the fathers of several other neighboring families and we thought sure my dad would be picked up next because in those days they had a kind of community organization, just for Japanese, because our parents couldn't join anything else. And I'm sure it's that list the FBI grabbed--and any name on there would be picked up--although my dad wasn't active at that particular time. That's probably the only reason they didn't pick him up. But he had his little bag ready for him by the front door. We woke up every morning afraid that he was gone. We were lucky − — they didn't take him, because some of the families that were left had small children.*

TESTIMONY OF AMY IWASAKI MASS, LOS ANGELES, AUGUST 8,1981

By nightfall and through the next tense weeks, the FBI rounded up leaders of the Japanese community considered a security risk. Anyone connected to Japanese businesses, newspapers, government or those who visited Japan frequently. They took Buddhist and Christian church leaders, fishermen, storekeepers, teachers, without charging them of any crime. Many were held in federal prisons for the duration. Their crime? Looking like the enemy.

NORM, ELEMENTARY SCHOOL STUDENT

Norman Mineta was the youngest in his family. He had three sisters and a brother, all much older that Norman: Aya was 25, Etsu was 24, Helen was 21, and Albert was 17. Norman had just turned 9 when the war began. It was a frightening time. Even happy family occasions were hard to plan.

The Mineta family. Norm is in the white shirt in the front row.

My oldest sister, Aya was getting married in March of 1942 in San Francisco. We were living in San Jose, so we had to have a permit from the FBI because there was a curfew from 7PM to 7 AM. If you travel more than 50 miles, you had to have a permit. [This was] before everybody went off to camp. We couldn't travel in groups larger than five, so my brother had to stay at home and the rest of us were able to drive up to San Francisco. I remember, we were coming back from San Francisco and it was about 6:45 and we were still maybe 20 mins. to a half hour away from home. We were all worried. What if we get caught? What will they do to us? So, my dad said, "Well, now, Norman, you keep looking out the back window—for police." My dad was trying to hurry home to get us home before the curfew, which we were able to do without being stopped by the police.

HON. NORMAN MINETA, SEC OF TRANSPORTATION
INTERVIEW WITH JFO 10/14/04

"NONE ARE TO BE TRUSTED"

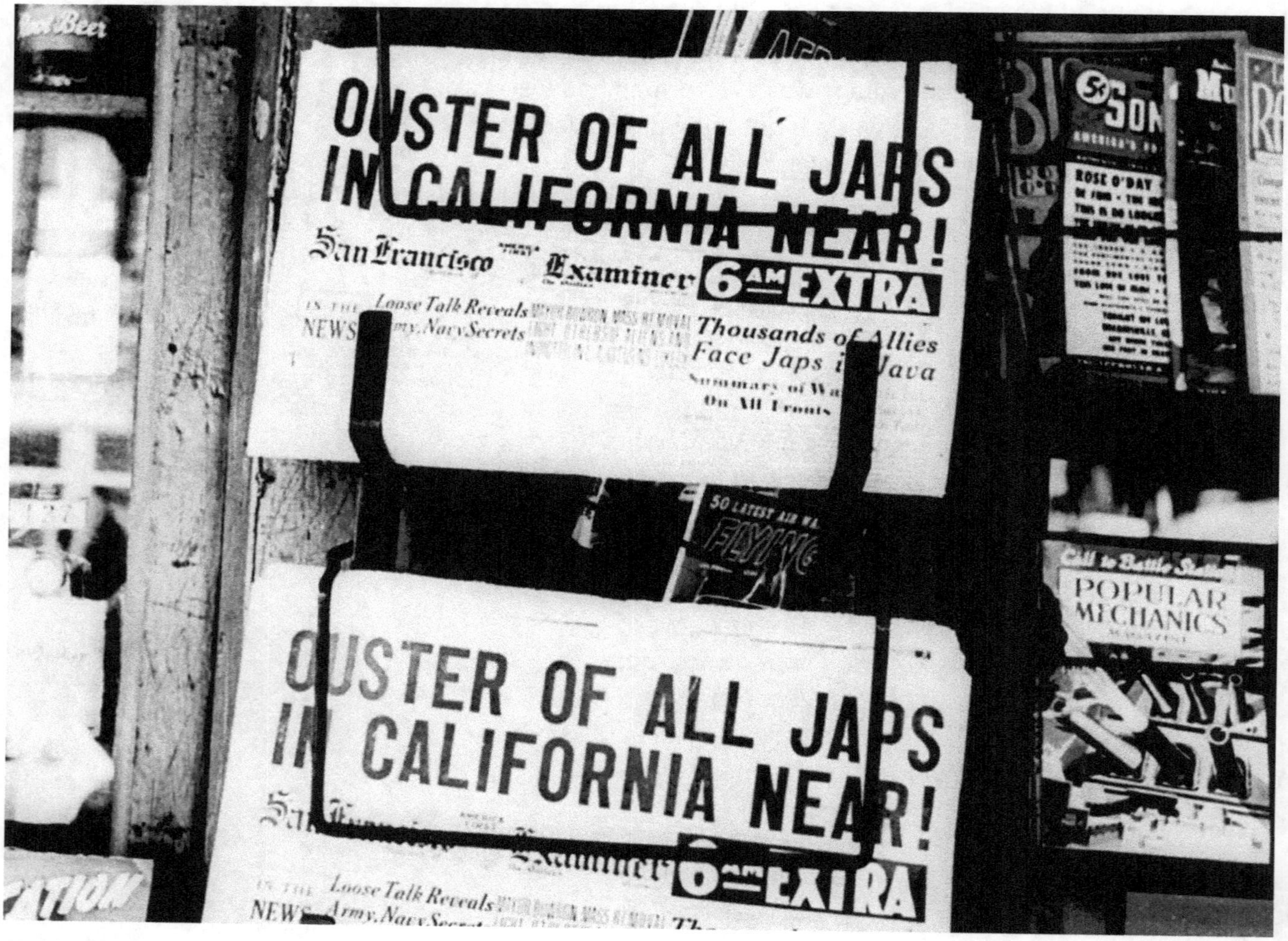

General John DeWitt

On February 19, 1942 President Franklin Delano Roosevelt issued Executive Order 9066, setting the stage for the mass removal of all Nikkei from the "war zone" as defined by the War Department and military leaders of the area, chiefly General John DeWitt.

YOSH, COLLEGE AGE STUDENT

All Packed Up and Ready to Go

The newspapers were bad, but what's worse, the government went along! They did nothing to protect our rights. In February, the 19th to be exact, the President signed a piece of paper— Executive Order 9066—declaring most of the West Coast a military zone and our fate was sealed. He put us in the hands of the army and General John DeWitt, Commander of Western Defense, who had nothing but contempt for all of us! The war just gave him the excuse to act on his hatred. He's the one who came up with that memorable line, 'A Jap's a Jap' or as he put it...

"The Japanese race is an enemy race and while many second and third generation Japanese born on U.S. soil, possessed of United States citizenship, have become "Americanized", the racial strains are undiluted".

According to that nit-wit, DeWitt...sending us away from the coast was a "military necessity." With him running the show, it wasn't any question of if—only when.

YOSH KUROMIYA INTERVIEW WITH JFO, 10/21/05

HATE IN THE PRESS

"I am for evacuating EVERY Jap, alien or native Jap of any kind over 700 miles from any coast and there...under guard."

"Move them back in the desert and feed them rice."

"None are to be trusted. They are a treacherous people."

"We want to see them all sent back to Japan where they belong and leave America for Americans."

"Did God mark the Jap as he did the snake, so no mistake could be made of his kind: Look at the Jap's eyes, listen when he speaks...did you hear the hiss before the words left his mouth? Were his eyes made slanting and the hiss put between his lips to warn us to be on guard?"

LETTERS TO EDITOR
SANTA ROSA PRESS DEMOCRAT 1/18/42

WAITING FOR A SIGNAL FROM HOME

Theodore Geisel, later known as Dr. Seuss, was liberal in his thinking except when it came to the Japanese Americans. In "Waiting for the Signal From Home," PM Magazine, February 13, 1942 he portrays the Nikkei as traitors.

A U. S. Army soldier, a member of military police, posting
official notices for the forced departure of all men, women and
children of Japanese descent, aliens and non-aliens (aka US
citizens) from the military zone on the West Coast.

ARTHUR, COLLEGE AGE STUDENT

*In April, I saw posted on the
telephone poles and the
storefronts...orders for all persons
of Japanese ancestry, to prepare
for mass evacuation from the West
Coast. My initial reaction was one
of outrage. They can't do that to
me. I am an American citizen. My
parents taught nine children to be
obedient to parents, to superiors,
their country. Thus, we complied to
this order, herded meekly as lambs
into an American concentration
camp.*

TESTIMONY OF ARTHUR MAKOTO TSUNEISHI
LOS ANGELES, AUGUST 5,1981

ROBERT, ELEMENTARY SCHOOL STUDENT

I was just 10 years old when I became suddenly a squint-eyed yellow-bellied Jap' to my fourth-grade schoolmates, who had formerly been my friends. I vividly remember the agony of hiding behind the barn and crying after returning home from school and being unable to tell my father. I could see that he was shattered and confused by the order that our family was to pack what we could carry and be taken to what the Government called a relocation center.

I vividly remember wartime propaganda posters and newsreel accounts about the 'sneaky, treacherous, rapacious, yellow-bellied Japs' who were the enemy. Nobody in the Government made distinctions between the 'Japs' of the Japanese Imperial Army and me. I was one of the enemy, though 10 years old, and placed in a concentration camp.

TESTIMONY OF ROBERT MOTEKI, NEW YORK, NOVEMBER 23,1981

BUDDY, JR. HIGH STUDENT

Buddy Takata's parents were sharecroppers. His dad was a Nisei born in Hawaii; his mom was a picture bride brought from Japan in 1920. They lived in a small farming community in the small city of Campbell, where there was a cannery for Campbell's soup. All his classmates, teachers, and even the principal wouldn't talk to Buddy after Pearl Harbor.

I almost got my Dad into trouble. In 1942, I was a very active scout trying to climb the ranks.

Troop meetings were every other Wed night from 7 to 9 PM. But the curfew for Japanese Americans was 8 PM. I was Gung-ho to go to the troop meeting, even though it took me half hour to walk home. So, I violated the curfew by about an hour and a half. I did that for a couple of meetings—then all of a sudden, one of the boys told his father that I was out beyond curfew. Next thing you know, the FBI shows up at our door and quizzing my parents — "What is your son doing out after curfew? Spying? Plotting? Scheming?" And my dad says, "No! He thinks he's this all-American boy trying to climb the ranks of scouting. I didn't think there was anything wrong being out a little beyond curfew, so I let him go." Well, the FBI was satisfied with what my dad said. But we often wondered what would have happened to him if he were an Issei, an immigrant? Would he have been taken away to one of the Department of Justice camps? I was a bad boy scout — not obeying the military law.

BUDDY TAKATA INTERVIEW WITH JFO 11/07/04

Close-out sales were everywhere in LA's Little Tokyos and other cities up and down the west coast.

I belonged to the Boy Scouts of America, Troop 52, made up mostly of Nisei. We had regular meetings soon after the war began...we were playing "Midnight Football" a game which entails switching lights on and off, and we were playing in the local elementary gym.

The next day the school principal received calls from people in the vicinity, accusing us of signaling to Japanese War planes.

We disbanded, never to meet again.

TESTIMONY DR. J. HIRABAYASHI, SAN FRANCISCO, AUG 13,1981

YOSH, COLLEGE AGE STUDENT

We knew it was coming...the so-called evacuation. The newspapers were saying we could show our loyalty by going along and not making a fuss. Heck, we should have refused from the start. But, no, it was those geniuses from the Japanese American Citizens League, the JACL that sold us out! Listen, they had a hand in the FBI roundups! They were the ones who helped make the A-B-C list of so-called suspects! What a bunch! They held themselves out as 'real' Americans, not like their immigrant parents. Those idiots thought they were so brilliant! They kept telling everyone to cooperate with the government...if we wanted to be accepted by America. You gotta look to the future they insisted. Some future they gave us!

Up 'til the war, the Issei men, our immigrant fathers, were respected as the wise leaders of our community. But not anymore. Those geniuses tried to tell us that we'd be safer, going into the camps than staying here in what the army called the military zone. Can you believe that? They also told us if we didn't go they'd take us anyway, so there was no choice...we should go along and show our patriotism.

We left our homes, our cars, our businesses, the lives our Issei parents had built with backbreaking labor! We even believed that the government would keep its promises and store our possessions. By the time we walked through the gates, with soldiers holding guns with bayonets, we knew it was all a pack of lies.

YOSH KUROMIYA INTERVIEW WITH JFO 10/21/05

NELS SMITH, GOVERNOR OF WYOMING

Out on the West Coast they were doing everything in their power to get the Japanese Americans moved away from the coast. But it was not that simple. There were rumors that the government was going ship them all to Wyoming. That spring Governor Nels Smith gave a fiery speech saying...

People in [my] state have a dislike of any Orientals, and simply will not stand for being California's dumping ground. If the government permits the Japanese to travel freely and settle where they please in Wyoming, then before long...There would be Japs hanging from every Pine tree.

NELS SMITH, WRA SPEECH, APRIL 7, 1942

Racist Anti-Japanese messages were everywhere. It was open season on hate!

IKE, HIGH SCHOOL STUDENT

Ike Hatchimonji hated his Japanese name, Tasuke, which literally translated means "help," because kids would tease him and call his name to help them – just as a joke. His father was a successful businessman in El Monte who started his own retail business selling seeds to farmers. Ike and his twin brother Mike were 14 when the war began. He was active in scouts and played the bass drum.

We experienced going to a segregated school in El Monte. The Latino and Asian kids all went to one school, the Lexington School, a run-down place. We had to walk about half a mile and then take a bus the rest of the way to that segregated school. The white kids went to Columbia Street School, which was supposed to be better. So, my parents went to the principal of the Columbia Street School and asked why we couldn't be transferred over—and they refused. But at the same time, the principal of the Mountain View School happened to be there in the office, and he said, "I'll take your kids." So, we were transferred to the other school—out of district I suppose, so from the 2nd half of 2nd grade till 8th grade, we went to that school. Now the ironic part about this situation is that we lived just across the fence from the Columbia Street School!

Our principal, when he learned of our evacuation, called Mike and me into the office. We were scared stiff—what did the principal want to see us for? And he said he apologized for the fact that we had to leave before the end of the school term. He understood it wasn't right and wanted to say how sorry he was to see us being forced to leave. I'll always remember that act of kindness.

IKE HATCHIMONJI INTERVIEW WITH JFO 11/04/04

The Hatchimonji Family on the day of departure, May 1942. From left to right: Tasuke Ike, Megumi Mike, Kumezo father, Nobue mother, and daughter Gloria, wearing family ID tags.

NOB, JR. HIGH STUDENT

Selling precious possessions for next to nothing was heart wrenching. Valuables had to be sold or abandoned.

I watched my parents' despair. The army was giving us a week or less to pack up and leave. I remember things like the refrigerator and the piano... and a buyer who offered $25 for the piano. He said all he had was ten dollars but maybe he could borrow the rest from his relatives—but it turned out he couldn't get the rest of it. He took both for ten dollars. And we had a washing machine and refrigerator, which at that time, we had to save a long time to just buy one of those...Dad put the car in storage. We just didn't know how long the duration would be and then it wasn't long before the price of the rental space was worth more than the car—so, we lost the car too. Dad had to sell his business.

Nobuyuki Shimokochi phone interview and emails with JFO 11/12/04

FRANK EMI

We had about $25,000* invested in our supermarket, in fixtures and produce. That was a lot of money then. We had only a week to sell it — the best we could get for it was $1500. We took a real shellacking! People knew they had us over a barrel. There was one guy who came in and made such an insulting offer I wanted to throw him out.

FRANK EMI INTERVIEW WITH JFO 10/20/05

*That 25,000 would be the equivalent of more than $400,000 today.

JOY, HIGH SCHOOL STUDENT

Joy Teraoka grew up in LA where her family had one of the first modern dry-cleaning establishments on 8th Street. Joy was in the 10th grade at Polytechnic High. Her sister was at Belmont High. Singing has always been something Joy loved doing—in school, in church, among friends.

We had to leave behind old photo albums from my great-grandparents' era to our own, Japanese kimonos and obi, my grandmother's hand-drawn flower arrangement book, antique scrolls, and our piano, sewing machine, refrigerator, and such. But, my saddest memory was having to leave our dog, Rexy. (Joy pauses, the memory wells up.) We were not allowed to bring pets. My parents arranged for one of their customers to take Rexy, our dog. Anyway, when Rexy was transferred to the new owner's car to be driven away, he balked at going and was bewildered with what was happening to him. It was soooo sad...Rexy, was just as inconsolable as we were when those strangers hauled him away.

JOY TAKESHITA TERAOKA INTERVIEW WITH JFO 6/9/05-9/10/05

SAM, HIGH SCHOOL STUDENT

On the last day that I attended school, I walked all the way home. I had to walk through my hometown to get home and I remember whistling out loud the Marine Hymn to show everyone that I was an American—but nobody cared.

Sam Nakagawa, Troop 333 Book

"I was an AMERICAN—
but nobody cared."

NANCY MATSUMOTO

Like most Sansei, or third-generation Japanese Americans, I was born years after the end of World War II. I grew up knowing next to nothing about my family's wartime imprisonment. Sure, I heard occasional stories about 'camp,' usually funny stories about neighbors, or youthful adventures. But I didn't understand the violent nature of our family's sudden uprooting, and the desolate, difficult conditions they endured. This was no summer camp. I was well into high school, college and beyond when I began to question those stories and digging deeper, in search of the truth.

My Aunt Terry told me about how getting ready for the evacuation was so rushed, emotional and full of trepidation; families had no idea where they would be sent. She remembered, 'We all bought boots before we went to camp. There was a big scare; they're going to put us in this place with big snakes and you have to protect your legs!' So, the sale of boots soared. In the high desert of Wyoming's Heart Mountain, it wasn't snakes, but snow they needed boots for. 'I remember going to school in snow... up to my knees, plowing through the drifts to get to school...it was a good thing we had them,' my aunt recalled.

"Getting ready for the evacuation was so rushed, emotional and full of trepidation..."

E-DAY—"EVACUATION DAY"

Evacuation was the euphemism the government used for the forced mass removal of over 120,000 men, women, and children of Japanese Ancestry. Evacuation was a prettied-up word, meant to imply that they were protecting Japanese Americans. In fact, it was an E-Day—an Expulsion, an Exile, and Exclusion.

KAZ, ELEMENTARY SCHOOL STUDENT

Right there at the corner there were all these families with their bags and bundles and all the buses are all just parked in the road. We were allowed to carry just one suitcase per person, so my mother got these big suitcases 'cause she wanted to stuff in as much as she could take. And here we were, this is after my dad was taken away...I was the oldest, in sixth grade and then my sister was in fourth grade, and my brother was in the second grade, and we're all lugging these heavy suitcase to the point of departure. It was several blocks from the temple to the bus that was going to take us to Santa Anita. And I remember a woman pulled up and gave us a ride. It was just few blocks, but I remember that.

My little brother and sister were terrified when they saw the soldiers shouting orders. I swear they must have sent the tallest guys in the Army that day—they looked like giants—giants with guns!

KAZ SHIROYAMA INTERVIEW WITH JFO 11/7/04

"My little brother and sister were terrified."

AMY, ELEMENTARY SCHOOL STUDENT

I was six years old...I remember the scared feeling I had as we lined up to go into the buses to take us to the assembly centers. We all wore tags with numbers. Each family lined up with the oldest member of the family at the head of the line, the youngest at the end. I was scared; I was the youngest and I wanted to be closer to my parents.

TESTIMONY OF AMY IWASAKI MASS
LOS ANGELES, AUGUST 6, 1981

Grandmother and two girls wearing identification numbers on tags are waiting for evacuation bus.

STAN, HIGH SCHOOL STUDENT

I shall remember that day that I was evacuated for the rest of my life. I shall remember how I stood on the corner of Garvey and Atlantic with about a thousand others – then the buses came and whisked us off to camp. I shall remember the lump which came into my throat as the bus went down the street and when some of the people on the sidewalks and Mexican laborers in the field waved to us.

STANLEY HAYAMI DIARY, MAY 4, 1943,
HAYAMI FAMILY PAPERS, JANM

Leaving their homes, friends and their liberty.

With rope-tied make-shift bundles, farm families board evacuation buses with personal treasures.

IMPRISONED: SO-CALLED ASSEMBLY CENTERS

MARJORIE, COLLEGE AGE STUDENT

> *The clanging of the steel gate behind us as we disembarked is a sound I will never forget, for it changed our lives forever...as that gate clanged shut, I realized I was imprisoned without a single criminal charge against me, and without the benefit of due process of the law. I was there solely because I was Japanese. My birth right as a United States citizen meant absolutely nothing.*

TESTIMONY OF MARJORIE MATUSHITA, LOS ANGELES, AUGUST. 5,1981

"There I was, a girl of 19 years, native-born American, declared a menace or a spy or possible saboteur...without any chance to defend myself. "

TESTIMONY OF AKIYO DELOYD, LOS ANGELES, AUGUST 4, 1981

"I remember...the guard towers, the soldiers with their guns pointed in to us...Weren't they supposed to be protecting us from all the potentially dangerous hostile people outside?"

TESTIMONY OF AMY IWASAKI MASS, LOS ANGELES, AUGUST 6, 1981

YOSH, COLLEGE AGE STUDENT

Well, we were only supposed to take what we could carry and I guess people complied. But there were a few of us, people like us, that decided, well what's the big deal, if we're going to be there we might as well be comfortable. So, we loaded up the truck and took all sorts of things because we decided, well if we can't use it, some poor person, somebody could use it. We never dreamt that we were going to be shifted further inland later on. When we reached the gate they told us, 'Grab what you can carry off the truck.'

"So, we loaded up the truck and took all sorts of things because we decided, well if we can't use it, some poor person, somebody could use it."

Through the chain link fence we could see the trucks and cars were still there in the parking lot— and then all of a sudden, they all disappeared! We never saw our stuff or the truck again. I heard later that they just destroyed a lot of cars and trucks that people came in. That was pretty dumb, considering that with a war on, no new cars or trucks were being built for civilians. I don't know if my dad ever got any compensation for the truck. I kind of doubt it, because we were disobeying orders, so it's our own fault, they'd say.

YOSH KUROMIYA INTERVIEW WITH JFO, 10/21/05

BUDDY, JUNIOR HIGH SCHOOL STUDENT

We were living in a horse stable. The army called it an apartment! Well, a stable consists of two rooms and we had a family of ten so there are five in one stall and five in the other. And what were some of the worse things? Well, first the stench! From the animals--they just couldn't get rid of that. Even though we had grown up around horses, we had horses on the farm, but still the stench was terrible.

BUDDY TAKATA INTERVIEW WITH JFO 11/07/04

They were living in horse stables that still smelled of former tenants.

NORM, ELEMENTARY SCHOOL STUDENT

Ten-year old Norman Mineta wore his scout uniform to the train when he and his family left their home in San Jose. His father, who came to America as a boy of 14, was a successful insurance agent. But soon after the war began the state of California suspended his license. Like other Issei, he became an enemy alien.

My dad loved this country very, very, much and I only saw him cry on three occasions: one was on the 7th of December 1941, the other was on May 29th 1942 and that was the day that we were boarding the train to go off to camp and the other, the third time, was in June of 1956 when my mother passed away. My dad on the 7th of December 1941 couldn't understand why, as he said, the land of his birth was attacking the land of his heart.

When I boarded the train I had my baseball, baseball glove and baseball bat and as I got on the train the MPs confiscated the bat on the basis it could be used as a lethal weapon.

We were among the last to go into camp, May 29th. The army commandeered all the racetracks and fairgrounds in Washington, Oregon, and California because they had built – in living quarters, namely—stables. But by the time we got down to Santa Anita all the stables had been taken up so we lived in the barracks that had been built in the parking lot of Santa Anita racetrack...we were fortunate.

When we got there, the first thing we did was to make our own mattress. I remember stuffing that mattress ticking with straw and my father said, "That's not enough straw to make it a comfortable mattress." He kept telling me to jam more in and of course, the more I jammed in, the heavier it was going to be for me to carry this thing.

We used to stand by the fence near our barracks where we lived. The Arcadia Theatre was right across the street and they'd have their marquee with whatever movie was playing and we'd sit there saying, "Boy wouldn't that be nice to be able to go see the Lone Ranger or whatever film was showing there. But then, of course, along here, every two or three hundred feet along this barbed wire fence there are guard towers with searchlights and machine guns.

I remember those search lights that would go back and forth, and you know, I'd pull the blanket over my head and even as I closed my eyes I could still feel that search light going back and forth, back and forth, even though I was under that blanket and trying to get to sleep.

HON. NORMAN MINETA, SEC OF TRANSPORTATION INTERVIEW WITH JFO 10/14/04

"My father said, "That's not enough straw to make it a comfortable mattress. He kept telling me to jam more in."

BILL, JUNIOR HIGH SCHOOL STUDENT

Bill Shishima attended the Maryknoll School in LA, a Catholic school with one Chinese American and one Filipino—all the rest were Japanese Americans. His father had a grocery store with mostly Mexican customers. His mom was more fluent in Spanish than English, a business necessity.

In the middle of the night, when we had to use the bathroom, when we came outside—the spotlight would pick us up and follow us wherever we're going. And then when you came outside the bathroom, it's waiting for us and followed us back. But us kids, sometimes we'd just detour and go behind or closer to the barracks so it won't pick us up. We figured they can't do anything to us! That was our game—we played hide and seek with the spotlights.

BILL SHISHIMA
INTERVIEW WITH JFO 11/05/04

Santa Anita Guards with their guns and spotlights were not playing games, but they did inspire some late-night games, proving that boys will be boys.

BUDDY, JUNIOR HIGH SCHOOL STUDENT

From the time we reported to the train depot in Santa Clara to go to Santa Anita... from that time on we were guarded...all the time...by soldiers with rifles and bayonets. I wasn't frightened, but I felt we had lost our freedom and all our Constitutional rights...here we are just finishing 8th grade, studying U.S. History and the Constitution and I said, 'I don't have to worry. I have my rights and I haven't done anything wrong...And my father, being a Nisei, felt that way, and yes, my mother, too. She's an immigrant, but she's a legal resident, so she's protected by the Constitution, yet that didn't help.

BUDDY TAKATA INTERVIEW WITH JFO 11/07/04

SUTTER, HIGH SCHOOL STUDENT

Sutter Kajita's mom died when he was 2 ½, so his dad raised the family. They lived in Sacramento and were sent to a quickly built small assembly center, Walerga, just outside the city.

A Monopoly Party!

We stood on long lines for everything...to eat, to get a shot, to go to the bathroom. The day we got there... we waited forever on a line just to check in—and then they stamped a number on my wrist! And the soldier says, 'Now this is more important than anything! More important than your name—forget your name!'

As a kid you wonder, what is this? Will it come off? And it was getting toward evening when we finally found our barrack. It was new, but there were weeds growing through the bottom of the floor and one light bulb in the middle. It was dark in there so we opened the windows to try and let some light in and we see there is nothing in here except some old folded up cots and in the corner there were some mattresses. My father was opening them up and he realized that those were not mattresses—they were hay mattresses; that really upset my dad.

That's when it struck me very hard. He got one of the cots out and we're all sitting on it. My older sister, my brother, and I sat next to her and she just burst out crying. That was a bad night for us until there was a knock on the door and there is the Nagaishi family! Shorty, one of our group, and his older brothers and Kimi, their older sister, was there and she said, 'Hi guys, why don't you come over to our house?' She could see we were crying. But, we went over to their place which was about two or three barracks down and the door opens and they are having a party! A Monopoly party! Honest to God, we were so happy! We were smiling. It was so bad—but they really helped us out! I always remember that.

I owe those people a lot for that.

SUTTER KAJITA TELEPHONE INTERVIEW WITH JFO 3/14/05

MIKE, HIGH SCHOOL STUDENT

Mike Hatchimonji was 14 and lived in El Monte, east of Los Angeles when the war began. His father, a successful businessman had come to America as a young man and attended Columbia University while working as a houseboy. Before the war, Mike and his twin brother Ike attended a school that was almost entirely Caucasian. At the time, there was a comic strip called Mike and Ike; They Look Alike. That's when, they got "hung" (as Mike put it,) with their names, even though they were fraternal twins not identical. Not only didn't they look alike, they didn't think alike, either.

We were taken to the Pomona Assembly Center, not far from where we lived. What a cultural shock! I never realized there were so many Japanese people and that so many of them didn't speak English!

The barracks were very shoddy, with large cracks in the walls and the opening in the ceiling where you could hear every sound. The food—terrible. But I remember one occasion when we

"A double fence so you couldn't actually come in contact with a person."

had visitors, our old neighbors, the Mills family came once to visit us. There was a compound outdoors with a double fence so you couldn't actually come in contact with a person. But Mrs. Mills left a box of fried chicken for us. That was a rare treat. So, my brother and sister and I took it back to the barracks and devoured it!

Here we're eating like animals—ravenously—and my mother was really upset, very saddened by that.

MIKE HATCHIMONJI INTERVIEW WITH JFO 11/04/04

FRANK, COLLEGE GRAD

Eldest of four children, Frank spoke only Japanese with his parents until he started school. After that, as in the following letter to Mike Mackey, he insisted that his little brothers and sister speak English so that when they went to school they would have an easier time. He often played the part of surrogate parent – negotiating their world outside the home.

> *My full name is Frank Yutaka Hayami and I was the oldest of four children. My father gave us all an American name because he wanted us to grow up as full-fledged American citizens. Then he gave us a Japanese middle name because he feared that he might be forced to return to Japan with his family because of the anti-Japanese feelings in those days in California and the fact that Japanese nationals were not eligible for American citizenship, nor were they permitted to purchase land or enjoy the other benefits of full American life. Of course, later on my parents were permitted to send their American sons into battle for the cause of liberty while they were being detained in the camp, denied the right to return to their home in California and denied the right to US citizenship afforded to all European nationals.... Sorry...I didn't mean to get on the soap-box.*

> *I was about 22...in my fifth year at the Univ. of California in Berkeley majoring in Electrical Engineering when a foreign country, Japan, attacked my country, the United States, at Pearl Harbor and forever changed my life as it did to millions of others. Since I had enough credits, my diploma was mailed to me and I graduated college with Bachelor's degree in Engineering when the mailman threw the diploma onto my cot at camp.*

Left to Right: Stanley Tsuneo Hayami, Frank Yutaka Hayami, Grace Sachiki Hayami, known as "Sach", & Walt Mitsuru Hayami.

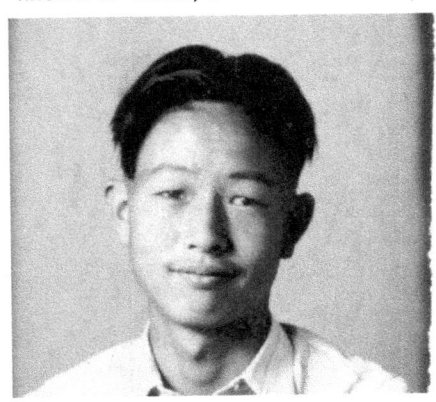

TAK, HIGH SCHOOL STUDENT

Takashi Hoshizaki was a student at Belmont High in Los Angeles. He liked building and flying gas-powered model airplanes. He was Boy Scout Scoutmaster of Troop 313 (Bacon Sakatani's troop) and was in the first class of graduates of Heart Mountain High in 1943.

Life was very, very hard on people. We were there in the late part of May, June, July and August and that year it was very, very hot! I worked in the mess hall. In order for people to come and eat they had to stand outside in a line and people were passing out. It was really bad, because more people were coming in than they had food for.

I was working in the kitchen and I remember there were thirty of us and we fed over 2,000 people. So, what do you do with the rice? You keep pouring water to it...so they each have a bowl of gruel and the only other thing I remember there are the big wheels of cheese. Well, the Japanese people hate cheese--and the only thing they got was a little sliver of cheese.

Like many WRA photos, this was posed to present a sunny image of plenitude in contrast to Tak's telling of the reality.

So that is some of what we went through. Privacy was not there—you know, high school students want a little privacy. But, no, it wasn't there at all. But the lack of privacy wasn't the only bad thing about the latrines. The latrine near our barrack used to overflow and a foul odor of sewage ran under the barracks.

I don't know if anyone mentioned the showers...For the fellows it wasn't bad – they were used to it from gym. But, for the women it was terrible. There were a half a dozen shower heads and that was all...no privacy there either...in some very extreme cases some women waited for two or three in the morning to take a shower.

TAKASHI HOSHIZAKI INTERVIEW WITH JFO 11/04/2004

NANCY MATSUMOTO

In Santa Anita, kids like my mom roller skated and played hopscotch, while older teens busied themselves with school clubs, sports and dances. My mom's friend Eiko Sakuda, who was nine when she got to camp, remembers, "We used to go to the mess hall and stand on those construction 'horses' and peek in and watch all the older kids dancing, the guys and the girls, and say 'Ha-ha-ha, look at them holding hands, that's so funny!'"

A certain segment of kids roamed the camp in packs with nothing much to do. It was fun for them at first, but it became clear they needed some kind of program. That's when a group of Nisei teachers and college age students got together and set up classes—they used the grandstands.

Most of them weren't really teachers and they didn't have any books and they had to share one great big space...but still, it kept the kids occupied. They even had assembly programs.

TOYO, TEACHER

At the first high school assembly, I witnessed an incredible incident! After the morning program was finished, as the students stood to return to their open classrooms, they began to sing God Bless America. These young people still believed in the country of their birth. We teachers could only gaze at each other, some of us with tears.

Testimony of Toyo Suyemoto Kawakami, chicago, september 22, 1981

YOSH, COLLEGE AGE STUDENT

I had plenty of questions, you know, like, why are they doing this? They have us all together here, so why don't they simply proceed with their hearings and determine at that point if they should still keep us there? Certainly, it had to be costing the taxpayers millions just to hold us there.

My dad was having a nice rest from all his hard-working years—except by then, of course, the whole idea of the family unit was beginning to break down. At home, at least one time in the day, in spite of how busy my parents were, for dinner, we'd all get together and have one meal together and then we'd play a game of cards or something. We had some kind of relaxation or entertainment as a family. Well, we lost that, but we weren't even aware of it initially because three times a day we would hear the "Clang!" of the mess bells--and we were told to line up for the mess hall, like cattle going from the barn to pasture. But even that started to fall apart, because after that we found other interests and we'd rather go eat with our friends. So, gradually the whole family structure fell apart.

Every night the bed checker would come to count heads. Imagine taking a job like that, spying on your own people. There were plenty who did it. But people didn't trust any of the Japanese who took such jobs inspecting the barracks and counting heads.... inu we called them inu...dogs!

Yosh Kuromiya interview with JFO 10/21/05

AMY, ELEMENTARY SCHOOL STUDENT

I remembered feeling bad about being Japanese, of being even able to speak Japanese, of having Japanese parents. I felt ashamed because I loved my parents. I also loved America. I get goose bumps when I sing the Star-Spangled Banner. I believed what our teachers taught about what a great country America is.

April 1942: Children of Weill public school in San Francisco saluted the flag every day, like schoolkids everywhere. But in a matter of weeks, Japanese American children would be forced to leave their school and friends. They would be imprisoned by their own country, though they were American citizens.

We were told that this was a patriotic sacrifice necessary for national security...The truth was that the Government we trusted, the country we loved, the nation to which we had pledged loyalty had betrayed us, had turned against us...Rather than facing the truth that America was being racist and unfair, we wanted to believe that America did not hate and reject us. This is the same defense that abused children use...Like the abused child who still wants his parents to love him and hopes that by acting right, he will be accepted.

Japanese Americans chose to be cooperative, obedient and quiet Americans—to cope with an overtly hostile racist America.

TESTIMONY OF AMY IWASAKI MASS, LOS ANGELES, AUGUST 6, 1981

EDITORAL, THE PACEMAKER (SANTA ANITA NEWSPAPER)

In spite of it all—Flag Day, on June 14, 1942 was no ordinary day. The nation dubbed it "MacArthur Day" in honor of General Douglas MacArthur, Commander of American Forces in the Pacific. It was a day dedicated to honoring heroes and an editorial in the Santa Anita camp newspaper, *The Pacemaker* shows that the Nikkei would not be left out. The editorial said...

We are denied an active role in this struggle,

but we, Americans, join other Americans in

honoring our heroes and our flag and our allies flags.

The American hero is our hero.

The American flag is our flag.

Even little children were marched around with flags that day and again on Fourth of July and all American holidays. Pint size patriots.

NOB, JR. HIGH STUDENT

Every Monday the police would come and do a shakedown inspection. Those awful Mondays. They were so dehumanizing. I felt so belittled...we had to drag everything we owned outside on the macadam pavement. They would go through everything you owned and take whatever they wanted. Straight razors, kitchen knives, carpenter tools, and whatever else they decided were contraband. I don't know for sure the real reason, but early in August there was a riot!

I heard it all started when the police confiscated electric hotplates that mothers brought to warm the babies' milk. There were milk stations that issued milk several times a day according to a preset schedule. But the babies wouldn't follow the same schedule. The mothers revolted and caused the riot—tension was high and it didn't take much to start a stampede. There were some injuries among people who were accused of being 'inu'(dog) or spies for the Army. There were a lot of rumors floating around all the time.

I don't recall shots being fired or that there were any injuries from gunfire. The soldiers came out with rifles with fixed bayonets, tear gas, and gas masks. The helmets and rifles were of WW I vintage. I don't recall seeing any of it used. I saw half track armored cars with machine guns ready to fire shiny copper jacketed bullets. I didn't see any tanks.

After the riot, there was an investigation. Turned out that Caucasian mess hall workers were stealing sugar and meat and selling it on the black market.

NOBUYUKI SHIMOKOCHI EMAILS AND PHONE INTERVIEW WITH JFO 11/12/04

There were all kinds of reasons given for the riot. It took days to quiet things down and some newspapers claimed it was proof they were not to be trusted, even though it was the guards who were to blame. Early in August rumors started. They were to be moving soon. They didn't know where they were to be taken. Only further away—inland.

Soon after the riot the second mass removal began. By the end of summer the assembly centers were closed and the Nikkei were all taken to one of the ten so-called "Relocation Centers." They sure did relocate — further inland, to places that must have been chosen for their cruel climate and utter desolation.

Barracks were under construction that summer of 1942. 2,000 workers put up barracks in approximately 60 days. Bottom line — they knew where their bread was buttered and having the camp was going to be good business. Nels Smith was voted out of office that year.

SHERIDAN PRESS

All that summer they were building what they called the "Jap Camp" just a few miles between Cody and Powell, right there in the shadow of Heart Mountain. They were putting up barracks so fast, you'd turn around and another of those buildings was hammered together. Sure it meant jobs for the community, but many were not happy about the new population. The *Sheridan Press* ran a few editorials with begrudging acceptance:

Somebody's Got To Take Them

We Don't Want any Japs Around Here! That's the first reaction one gets in asking about the possibility of our own region absorbing some of the Japanese who must be evacuated for the vital coastal regions. We agree. We don't want any Japs. But that doesn't help to solve the question. The question plainly and simply, is where can we put these Japs where they will have the least opportunity to do any harm to the United States of America? The answer, we are becoming convinced, is just as plain and simple as the question. It stands to reason that the Japs could do far less harm out here than they could living nearer to San Diego, LA, SF and Seattle.

We don't want them, it is true, and we should be given the promise that they will leave as soon as the war is over...but no sacrifice is too great if we are to win this war. The Japanese could take up the loss in farm labor that is growing increasingly serious, and they would become a factor in our economic business life. After all, they must live—and they must buy groceries. After all is said and done, we believe that this region will take them. There is no alternative.

SHERIDAN PRESS EDITORIAL, MARCH 8, 1942

DON, CODY BOY

In Wyoming, my dad got a job while they were building the camp out at Heart Mountain, that was before the Japanese people came. You know, it was a government construction and they had guards. You had to have a pass to get in. Dad worked the night shift and I would get to go with him and sleep in the car or the guardhouse. I was about 10 that summer. It was a hot one—and we kids, and I say we, because there were a few of us that did the same job; we'd go around where the carpenters, plumbers, and masons were working. Well, they didn't have soda cans in those days— they'd just drink their pop and throw their bottles down...our job was to go around and pick those bottles up and we'd turn them in for--I don't remember what we got-- maybe a penny a piece, but it was pretty good money to us kids. I remember, we'd see a bottle and we'd race — so we'd get it before the other guy could get it!

Don C. Easton, phone interview with JFO 12/17/04

10,000 JAPS TO BE INTERNED HERE
CODY ENTERPRISE, MAY 21, 1942

"We'd go around where the carpenters, plumbers, and masons were working...and pick those bottles up...we got maybe a penny a piece...pretty good money to us kids."

SECOND FORCED REMOVAL

IKE, HIGH SCHOOL STUDENT

We walked from the camp to a nearby rail siding...there were soldiers on both sides with what you call riot guns or shot guns that were sawed off—really unnecessary. I guess that's the way the military does things, but you know it's intimidating to see lines of soldiers with riot guns every ten yards or so, on both sides of you, as you are just walking down to the train...I don't recall much about the train trip. But I remember ... My father was sitting by himself and I went up to talk to him and he snapped at me. He never did that.

IKE HATCHIMONJI INTERVIEW WITH JFO 11/04/04

TEACHERS

By late summer, the WRA was enlisting a staff of teachers willing to work in the camps.

I was working on my Master's Degree in Colorado when I heard about a job teaching Social Studies at Heart Mountain.

I was grateful that my family controlled their tongues about the job I wanted to take. My brother was in the Navy, in the Pacific, on board a destroyer and my father was at home knowing that I was teaching in a Japanese camp trying to make life sensible for the people there. Everyone had a chance to do what they thought was the right thing to do. My brother volunteered and so I'm sure that's why my dad thought I should too.

For a lot of us, this was our first job. But there were a few who were already teaching and they were warned, 'If you leave our school to teach those Japs you will never be able to teach in our school system again.' One teacher told me how she was ridiculed by a lot of her neighbors back home...they couldn't understand why she would want to go teach children of the enemy!

It took real courage to come into the camps.

ALBERTA KASSING, JEAN MORTON QUINT, AND IRENE RATCLIFFE
PHONE INTERVIEWS WITH JFO 2004

A few of the teachers in the 1944 Tempo Heart Mountain Yearbook.

YOSH, COLLEGE STUDENT

I had never been on a train before! It was slow, the cars were pretty rickety but it was fascinating. I guess we went up into Ogden and into Idaho. We had no way of knowing where we were. There were no announcements. They weren't telling us and there were no street signs or anything. But I just guessed from the landscape and we started getting into the tree line with forests--beautiful country!

The Kuromiya family's identification number for the duration—5445.

Then we stopped and they added 2 or 3 more engines and sure enough we started going over an incline and I thought-this must be the Rockies! The train started weaving around the hillsides and you can see both ends of the train--the locomotives at the front and the locomotives they had put on the back, pushing and pulling at the same time. You look out and there's a deep ravine and next to you, you see the treetops! It was beautiful! Probably the most exciting trip I ever had until that time and then we saw some snow when we hit the summit and, of course, we started coming down again.

It began to get drier and drier and drier and of course, it was sagebrush and just flatness. We must have been going through Montana then. We headed south and further down into Wyoming.

The further we went the worse it got and then we stopped! In the middle of nowhere! What are we stopping here for? There's nothing here!

YOSH KUROMIYA INTERVIEW WITH JFO 10/21/05 PHOTO COURTESY YK

ARRIVAL

Trains arrived day and night for the next days.

TOSHI, HIGH SCHOOL STUDENT

It was a World War I or older vintage train. It had musty, dusty mohair seats which were very hard and did not recline. At night, they turned on the gaslights. That's how old the trains were! Every seat was filled. The first night we tried sleeping sitting up in our seats. The second and third nights, we took turns curling up on two seat spaces.

Even then, it was much too uncomfortable to get much sleep. Every time the train stopped at a station; we were ordered to pull the blinds down. However, we always peeked to see where we were since we were not told anything about where we were being sent.

TOSHI N. ITO TO MIKE MACKEY

ADMINISTRATOR NELSON

John A. Nelson was an administrative officer and eventually became assistant project director. He worked at Heart Mountain from July 1942-June 1943 when he was drafted into the Army. His diary gives a different view of life inside the barbed wire fence.

August 11, 1942

Everything is excitement today and for the past two days. Our first residents arrive about midnight. We have really been cracking our shirts trying to get ready to receive them. We aren't ready. Everything is torn up. Business has to go on and we are just about run down, but they won't wait and so we must meet them. We are looking forward to an experience we probably will never forget. Tonight we will begin an experiment in making democracy work.

JOHN A. NELSON DIARY ENTRY, AUGUST 11, 1942

FRANK, COLLEGE GRADUATE

When I first saw Heart Mountain, my heart sank. Bleak, scrubby, dusty, barren, desolate. Not a tree in sight. Dust stirring in the breeze. And row on row of those somber tar-papered shacks that were to be our shelter for the duration, all surrounded by barbed wire fencing and guard towers standing tall at each corner with armed American soldiers, guarding American citizens.

Frank Hayami to Mike Mackey

"Bleak, scrubby, dusty, barren, desolate."

BABE, CODY HIGH SCHOOL STUDENT

We knew trainloads of people were coming and we all went out there and sat in our cars waiting. Dozens of cars and trucks were out there with people just sitting and watching.

The trainload that I remember came in late. Must have come in at two o'clock in the morning. It was very cold. The thing I remember is this one old woman, stepped off of the train holding a canary in a cage and she was very concerned—worrying about that bird—because it was so cold! And she took her coat off and wrapped it around the birdcage and that was something I remembered forever! It will always stick in my mind that she was more concerned about the bird than about herself.

BABE MARTOGLIO PHONE INTERVIEW WITH JFO 7/25/06

Dorothea Lange's photographs, and this one in particular, speak of the sorrow of the journey. Her pictures tell such a story of shame, that the government impounded them for years, hid them away like a dark ugly secret.

NOB, JUNIOR HIGH SCHOOL STUDENT

"But there was nothing there! No one lived in Vocation. It was just a train stop along the track. It felt like the end of the world!"

I was a real city kid, used to the hub-bub of downtown Los Angeles where my parents ran a mom-and-pop grocery store on Central Avenue...Maybe that's why I'll never forget my first sight of Heart Mountain. Let me tell you about when I first got off the train. There was this shelter beside the tracks that said "Vocation." It was just a roof and four posts that held it up, in case it was raining or something. Anyway, there was a sign and I'm thinking—Vocation? It didn't mean a thing to me. I didn't know what vocation meant. But in the many years that have passed, every time I see that word, vocation, I think about that little shelter. It apparently was the name of a village or something. But there was nothing there! No one lived in Vocation. It was just a train stop along the track. It felt like the end of the world!

NOBUYUKI SHIMOKOCHI
EMAILS AND PHONE INTERVIEW WITH JFO 11/12/04

NORM, ELEMENTARY STUDENT

The day we got there it was extremely cold and really windy and as we got off the train to get on the truck to take us to our barracks...the wind was blowing and you had sand and tumble weed just blowing around...it was really cold. None of us really had the kind of jackets or clothing to deal with this new element that we were now in...I've always wondered how much money the Sears Roebuck or Montgomery Ward catalogue made from purchases that were made from the camps. But that first day in Heart Mountain was really something.

The Minetas got off the train and climbed into open trucks on a cold windy day. Coming from California, few people had the warm clothes needed and winter's chill came early to Wyoming.

When we got off that train, I can still feel how cold it was and having that sand just hitting your skin. Then when we got to the barracks, of course, there is a totally empty room, except for a potbellied stove in the corner and because of this wind, a constant wind, the fine silt ... was everywhere!

We were Block 24 Building 7 Unit B. That's how you always said where you lived; you'd say 24-7-B but it was just a single wall with tar paper on the outside and the inside. Just 2 by 4's. In one unit there was my mother, my father, my brother, my sister, and myself.

Hon. Norman Mineta, Sec of Transportation, interview with JFO 10/14/04

IKE, HIGH SCHOOL STUDENT

We arrived toward evening and it was getting dark and there were all these people. They had trucks waiting for us to take us to the barracks. You got your truck assignment when you came off the train, I think. So, we loaded our suitcases on the back of this open truck and they took us to a barrack in Block 14. That wasn't our permanent barrack, but I remember walking in and lo and behold — there's a bat flying around inside the unit and oh, my gosh that frightened the dickens out of us! We're not used to seeing bats flying around in our home. Of course, they are harmless but still. Later, we moved to Block 27. All in all, it was a matter of...adapting to the situation. In the beginning, there were all these problems with the food and the bathing and the toilets.

Nancy's Aunt Terry and her Grandmother, Tomiko.

NANCY MATSUMOTO

My mother and her family were transported by bus to Heart Mountain, Wyoming, approximately 1,147 miles from Los Angeles. My grandmother later wrote of this desolate, high desert wasteland where she would spend the next three years, 'The Rockies could be seen in the far distance; the nearby mountains surrounding the camp were all rock mountains, without a

single tree or blade of grass. Among them was a mountain that stood high and slightly apart from the others. It had a wide and smooth slope with a summit that made one think of a badly shaped version of Mt. Fuji. We were told that this was Heart Mountain.'

TEACHERS

Some of us teachers got to Wyoming early, not that school was ready to open. But we were supposed to help when the trains came in.

When the evacuees arrived at Heart Mountain they were actually herded off the train, through the clearinghouse, and up into the project. Military police were pacing back and forth with their guns on their shoulders and one was walking up and down among the people with his billy club swinging.

It seemed that each time a train arrived we had either a severe dust or rainstorm.

The people were loaded onto open army trucks which were piled high with baggage, fathers, mothers, and little kids. Small babies were taken up in private cars to the hospital. Some babies coming off the trains had mumps and measles, and these were isolated immediately. All evacuees were given a preliminary examination so as to help prevent any epidemic.

The facial expressions of the children were ones of bewilderment. They did not seem to know what the score was. The parents acted bewilderedly too, but at the same time appeared to be exceedingly grateful for any courtesy shown to them. They seemed to be resigned to the situation and accepted it in the customary oriental way.

When I was working down at the tracks helping to receive the people, I simply felt that I wanted to sit down and cry. My reaction was one of extreme pity. It was a terrific emotional shock for me to see these people herded off the trains and into such terrible living conditions. It seems to me that a good portion of the appointed personnel reacted in much the same manner.

INTERVIEWS WITH JFO WITH ALBERTA KASSING 11/12/04 AND JEAN QUINT 10/11/04

ADMINISTRATOR HANSEN

So far, this description has omitted perhaps the most obvious thing about the physical appearance of the camp. No mention has been made of color. Every one of the hundreds of residential barracks, mess halls, recreational halls, and laundry latrines had black tarpaper walls and roofs. Later on when they got around to building it, the centrally located high school with buff walls and red roof stood out like an island in a sea of blackness.

"a sea of blackness...obviously created by decree." A. Hansen

When one looked out over the camp, the prevailing impressions were of mechanical orderliness, blackness and bleakness. To a newcomer, it seemed unreal. My first feeling that this community did not actually exist, that it was just a bad dream I was having, has pretty much subsided. I have decided it is real after all. Now when I look out over the project, it seems substantial enough, but it just shouldn't be.

Most settlements sort of grow out of the ground and look as if they belonged. This one looks stuck here; it doesn't fit the landscape; it is obviously created by decree. It hardly seemed that people could live there. They might stay there temporarily, using the facilities in order to subsist and survive, but not live.

People did live. The barracks became homes; not normal homes but homes nevertheless. The camp grew to be a community. Again, it is not a full-fledged community. But there was organization, collective sentiments, and even some civic spirit.

WRA COMMUNITY ANALYST REPORT, ASAEL T. HANSEN

ADMINISTRATOR NELSON

September 11, 1942. Our city really looks like something at night. Row on row of lights and from a distance it looks like a real city. It gives one a sort of queer feeling tho to look out over the area at night with all the lights on and then realize that the city houses a race of people who because of their race have been isolated from society under very trying and difficult conditions, and many of whom may never return to their original homes and property. War is a cruel thing. Seems that a man with his brilliant mind could find a humane substitute for war. Am afraid tho that as long as there are nations there will be war.

September 17, 1942 I've been colder than H- E - double L today. A terrible cold wind blowing in from the northwest with snow on the foothills. Everyone in the office, including me, has been shivering all day. We did get a couple fires going...I feel sorry for those poor Japanese who are in apartments with no heat and not enough bedding to keep them warm. Really, it's a crime.

JOHN A. NELSON DIARY ENTRY, SEPTEMBER 11 & 17, 1942

Estelle Ishigo from Lone Heart Mountain.

"Shabby shivering people stood on line for G.I. socks, underwear, coats and wool pants."

FRANK HAYAMI

Our living accommodations were very sparse. No running water, no toilet, no baths in our single 20 ft by 24 ft room housing 6 members of our family. The lack of privacy bothered the two female members of our family. This was solved by stringing ropes from the ceiling around their cots, and draping sheets from the rope to the floor creating some privacy.

FRANK HAYAMI LETTER TO MIKE MACKEY

Stanley Hayami's Ink Drawing, Heart Mountain at Night

Each barrack had six one-room "apartments" with a single light and coal-burning stove in each room. A family of 5–8 had a room 24' X 20'; smaller family lived in a room 16' X 20'. There were 30 "blocks"—all exactly the same. Each block had 24 barracks, in rows of six. Between the rows were service buildings—a mess hall and an H-shaped structure with a boiler room, a laundry room, and two latrines. The other half block was a mirror image. Between the halves there was a firebreak and two recreation halls. An open space was used for softball and basketball.

Cartoon by Stanley Hayami, Tempo 1944, Heart Mountain High Yearbook.

"They gave those jackets to everyone...they were shabby moth-eaten old jackets left over from World War I Navy surplus and they were all adult sizes... when I wore mine it looked like the jacket was walking!"
- SUTTER KAJITA

ADMINISTRATOR NELSON

And now that I am so sympathetic, I was given today the responsibility of approving all requisitions on the warehouse for work clothing. So, I immediately tighten up again and insist on knowing why they want work clothing. Why shouldn't they wear what clothing they have. When one gets a jacket they all want them. But tonight, I checked the stock records and find we have thousands of jackets so guess I can jar loose. It's cold. They are from the warm California climate and this is frigid to them. So, guess I'll jar loose and let them have their jackets.

JOHN A. NELSON DIARY ENTRY, SEPTEMBER 17, 1942

TAK, HIGH SCHOOL STUDENT

Well, being a boy scout, I looked at this place and see it's a great place! For me, Wyoming was like a big long-term camping spree. I expected to see cowboys and Indians riding across the high desert! Just like in the movies!

But for my sisters, it was a place of horror! One of their jobs was to keep the house clean and to keep the clothes clean and it was just one big mess. The dust would just come in and settle on everything. I remember one day, I came in and said, 'Oh it's not bad in here.' I sat down on the cot, but when I got up you could see the impression of my rear-end!

TAKASHI HOSHIZAKI INTERVIEW WITH JFO 11/04/2004

FIRST WEEKS

Parents told their children "Shikataganai" — what you can't change you must accept.

They said it, but they had trouble accepting it themselves. They couldn't help thinking of all they worked so hard to build. What would become of the fields they had planted? What would become of them all?

ADMINISTRATOR NELSON

At noon, the mess hall...ran out of meat and about a hundred and fifty of them had to get along on a half wiener and a small amount of potato each. It's a serious situation and just simply has to be corrected. Uncle Sam is taking a beating for a lot of the food bought for Heart Mountain. The Army is paying 45 cents for a dozen eggs that would cost less than 30 cents in a retail store. Of course, they are buying thousands of dozens and that should have cost less--not more!

JOHN A. NELSON, DIARY ENTRY,
SEPT 3,1942

I'm afraid there is going to be some trouble in the camp one of these days if the mess hall situation is not cleared up. A complaint from one of the mess halls tonight that they had no food for breakfast; that there wasn't enough for supper and that they had been eating frankfurters for three days. The reports have been too numerous to be without foundation. Some others of the staff are equally concerned.

JOHN A. NELSON, DIARY ENTRY,
SEPT 11, 1942

HEART MOUNTAIN SENTINEL

John A. Nelson -- Wizard of Finance

Upon encountering John A. Nelson, senior administrative officer, for the first time, one decidedly would not think him the calculating master of finance and budget but a scholarly gentleman of leisure.

Contrary to this first impression Nelson's ability in the field of finance has been tried and proven these many years since his entering the U. S. Forest service in 1926. From administrative assistant and budget officer of the Forest service in Ogden, Utah, he transferred to his present position at Heart Mountain.

In charge of one of the most exacting and important administrative positions, he has supervision over the budget, finance, procurement and administrative personnel departments.

Born in Gunnison, Utah, 36 years ago, Nelson was educated in Gunnison Valley High school and Henager Business college in Salt Lake City.

Consistent with his scholarly appearance, Nelson's favorite pastime is reading. Poetry by Stephen Vincent Benet and classical music are his most common means of relaxation after a hard day's work.

Courteous, discreet and experienced in his field, the indispensability of Nelson's work can be recognized by the popular slogan used by other administrative officials in the earliest days of Heart Mountain—"If you want it well done, let John do it!"

John A. Nelson, Senior Administrative Officer

John A. Nelson, Heart Mountain Sentinel, December 12, 1942

IKE, HIGH SCHOOL STUDENT

We kids solved our food shortage by going from block to block. We hit three mess halls for one meal! We had to eat very fast, but in those days they didn't have control over who ate where... later they had passes. Raiding several mess halls was something we laughed about later, but at the time, being hungry was no laughing matter.

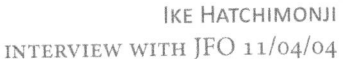

IKE HATCHIMONJI
INTERVIEW WITH JFO 11/04/04

NOB, JUNIOR HIGH SCHOOL STUDENT

While it seemed like such an awful place in the middle of the desert...it had its good points. We got a bed with cotton filled mattress instead of straw. Our room was a little bigger with a little more privacy. The toilets, lavatory, shower, laundry facilities, and mess hall were closer—a set for every 300 people (24 barracks). In Santa Anita, we stood in line under the hot sun while we waited our turned to get fed. It wasn't much of a hardship for us teenagers, but brutal to the elderly and mothers with small children. Latrines were further away and laundry and shower facilities were real far away. Doing the laundry was a real pain. We no longer had search lights flashing into your room all night.

Someone called it a city of lights in the desert, but it certainly wasn't like the usual. Each barracks had a light at each end, to help you find your way to the latrine at night. But in Wyoming, a lot of the locals actually envied us! They apparently envied our "indoor plumbing" although it was not exactly what you'd call indoors! We had to go out in the freezing cold to get to the latrine where there were flush toilets. The thing of it is, most farmers in that neck of the woods only had outhouses with a bench and a hole in the ground—no flush toilets. So they thought we were living in pure luxury. What a joke!

Nobuyuki Shimokochi, interview with JFO, 11/12/04

E. Ishigo
Sept. 4, 42.

by Estelle Ishigo from Lone Heart Mountain.

NANCY MATSUMOTO

My mother remembers the 'camp ladies' who worked in the mess halls, who would walk up and down between the aisles of tables with five-gallon cans of sugar. They would dole out one teaspoon of sugar to each person to sprinkle on their dry cereal. 'That was all you got, and I always wished I could have more!' she told me.

Inmates also lacked warm clothing due to delays in receiving clothing allowances, and had terrible problems keeping the barracks warm. The WRA built the barracks in such a rush they didn't let the wood dry or put up any insulation. Living with temperatures that plunged below freezing, they did what they could—by stuffing rags and newspapers into wood siding. But it didn't do much good.

Every room had a coal-burning stove. My mother's friend Yuki Yamashita recalls, 'We had this big pot-bellied stove. My mother used to get my little brother's diapers and warm them against the stove before putting them on him, it was so cold.'

Learning how to bank the coal in order to get a uniform fire that would last through the night—that was hard. More than one barrack caught fire when people put too much coal in the stove. It would turn cherry red and burn right into the floor! The only other problem was getting enough coal...people would take more than they needed for fear there might not be more.

KAZ, ELEMENTARY SCHOOL STUDENT

When the coal train came in you had to push and shove to get there before it was gone. There was a coal bin at each end of each block and we were in barrack one, right on the corner where the coal bin was. We had these little bushel baskets. I'd take a couple of those and load them up and pull them back to our front door on the sled. We would keep those bushel baskets full of coal, right outside our door. My mother always kept that fire burning. Right outside the window, all the families were building these little boxes that were their 'refrigerators' during the winter months. Just open the window and there it is—frozen stuff in a little box.

Collecting Coal

KAZ SHIROYAMA INTERVIEW WITH JFO 11/7/04

HEART MOUNTAIN SENTINEL

Most people think barbed wire fences surrounded Heart Mountain from the start, but, in fact, that came later. There were nine forty-foot guard towers that marked the outer limits of the camp. But, it wasn't until October that the MP's were ordered to build a barbed wire fence between each of the towers, a fence that would encircle the entire camp. The idea of a fence was another assault on their freedom. They called a meeting to stop its construction insisting that a fence was "unnecessary, immoral, and a gross violation of the most fundamental rights of citizens and law-abiding aliens."

Three thousand adult residents signed a petition that was sent to WRA Director, Dillon Myer in Washington. They argued that the fence was not only unnecessary, but "an insult to any free human being." The fence was proof that they were living in a concentration camp and were being treated as prisoners of war.

Their petition was ignored.

ADMINISTRATOR NELSON

One day last week a call came in from the MP office. They had thirty Japanese in the guardhouse...They were all kids except two and those two had been gathering rocks. The kids had been coasting on the hill near one of the guard towers and just outside the line. So they were picked up for having committed so great [a] crime as playing with their sleds. The poor little devils. It makes the heart bleed when one thinks of their condition and to think that while they are deprived of such pleasures, we are at the same time trying to teach them that this is a great democracy and that everyone regardless of race, color, or creed shall be treated equal.

It is an outrage to think that we must have a barbed wire fence around the Center.

We are doing something [that] will weaken their respect for America. They (the Nisei) have been generally strongly pro-American. But to be put in a corral as animals is going to make them wonder if it is worthwhile to remain loyal to the land [that] treats them as criminals and without benefit of trial puts them in a prison. All I can say is their emotions are becoming so strained that soon something is going to snap, and when it does---watch out.

JOHN A. NELSON, DIARY ENTRY, NOVEMBER 15, 1942

Not everyone had a real sled. Norman Mineta said, "What you do is get a box and you get inside it... and you let the wind carry you down...you're rolling inside the box...or you can flatten the box and just lay on top of it. We used to love getting in those boxes and being pushed by the wind...the wind was so fierce we'd just go rolling, rolling, rolling!"

DONALD, ELEMENTARY SCHOOL STUDENT

For kids from Southern California snow was an exciting novelty. It snowed theday after the Yamamoto family entered Heart Mountain in September 1942. Many more snowy days would follow. Donald and his pal, Kaz built sleds with wood scraps. Other kids used cardboard boxes.

Construction of the "camp" was basically finished and there were many pieces of scrap lumber left. With nothing else to occupy us, a group of guys made sleds from the lumber. Around November the snow was not covering the ground completely, but we looked for a place to go sledding. We found a gentle slope north-east of block 30, which was at the edge of the camp. The scant snow and loose dirt made sledding down the hill possible. There were other people (old men and young girls) watching us. After a couple of runs down the hill, vehicles with military policemen stopped at the bottom of the hill where there was a dirt road. We were ordered into the vehicles and taken to some barracks. It must have been the M.P.'s quarters. I don't think there were any jail facilities available.

Eventually, we were taken to a building in the administration area, We were told that we were out of bounds and that we should not have gone beyond the perimeter of the camp marked by wooden stakes that had red cloth attached. After the warning we were released and allowed to go. We were arrested for going under a fence that wasn't even there.

I don't remember if anyone was scared, more like apprehensive. There was a little girl about 7 years old with her older sister and the little girl was crying. I don't remember if I was scared. No one argued with the MPs, of course they had their weapons which they normally carried with them. We really didn't know why they were picking us up. I don't remember if I even told my family about this event.

The next day we went to see where the boundary of the camp was marked. The edge of the camp was marked by a 12-inch stake with the red piece of cloth attached. Well, we wanted our sleds. Taking a chance we ran down the hill, grabbed our sleds and ran back into camp. We didn't get caught.

DONALD YAMAMOTO INTERVIEW WITH JFO AT HM LAS VEGAS REUNION 10/04/05

JOY, HIGH SCHOOL STUDENT

There was no real school that first winter. We were compelled to go to classes in barracks like those we lived in. Usually, forty desks and seats were crowded into the tiny rooms. It was not considered the least bit ill-mannered to climb over desks to get to one's own seat...the congested traffic in the narrow aisles made it impossible to do otherwise. The cardboard walls were not soundproof, so if 'Miss Niland' was scolding 'Jim' in our room, it was heard from one end of the barrack to the other.

Ted Fujioka, second from left, student body president, with students gathered around the entrance to the principal's office.

In the winter we shivered ... the mercury dropped to 25 degrees below zero. Our sole source of heat was a small iron coal stove, which needed to be fed continually. Most of the girls wore slacks and boots. A familiar sight in camp— the ubiquitous mackinaw jacket over our 'Sears' or 'Monkey-Ward' catalogue-book-ordered dresses or trousers.

Before camp, we attended schools with only a handful of other Japanese Americans; we were a very small minority. In Heart Mountain, we went to a segregated school, almost all Japanese Americans. Although, it was harder to get good grades, since there were so many talented students; we were able to take leadership roles in school, roles that had been held largely by Caucasian students.

That year the student body elected its first president, a popular guy by the name of Ted Fujioka. I didn't really know Ted well outside of student government meetings, but he was what girls called —'huba-huba!' a real 'heart throb!' I was elected Student Body secretary, so I took the minutes at meetings where Ted presided. He was an all-American Boy— a serious, handsome, and articulate senior. An ideal example of a clean-cut, good student and born leader.

JOY TAKESHITA TERAOKA PAPERS AND INTERVIEWS 1/28/04

TEACHERS

Some came to class in cotton dresses, anklets, and short jackets even when the temperature was sub-zero. Others, whose parents could afford to send for winter things, came so heavily clothed it was a difficult task to 'de-sweater' them so that they would not be too warm. There were no bathrooms in the barracks, either. Students had to go outside to the latrines and stomp through the mud most of the winter. The soil was like clay that became exceedingly sticky. The slightest bit of water causes foot-deep mire which clings to the shoes and is brought into the classroom so that by the end of the day the floor was covered with dirt. All winter long there was dust in the classrooms.

Despite the lack of equipment, they got involved in activities they would have in their old schools, back home. They organized a school newspaper, a band, chorus, sports teams, and student government that kept them busy. They created a community that insulated them, in part, from the loss of their former lives. Outside of school they had clubs and dances, sports teams, and other social events. Sure, they missed home, but they were busy being teen-agers. They were typical students, full of life, eager to learn, and for the most part easy to work with in spite of the upsetting circumstances with which they and their families were coping. Some of the students liked to have fun with me such as hiding little lizards in my desk drawer, or a dead mouse, to scare me!

Most students were pretty accepting of the situation. But, there was one girl I will never forget. We were not supposed to talk about the incarceration, about the right and wrong of it, but one day I was asking students to share books and one of the girls started shouting, 'Why did they do this to us? Why weren't they prepared for us when we came to the camps? Why were we treated like animals?' Several times she said, 'Why weren't they prepared?' Finally, in order to stop her hysterics and gain control of the class I said, 'We were not prepared for Pearl Harbor, were we?' I regretted saying it as soon as the words were out of my mouth. The class acted as though each one had been slapped personally.

BASED ON COMMUNITY ANALYSIS SECTION, SEPTEMBER. 1,1943,
AND JFO INTERVIEWS WITH SCHOOL TEACHERS, WRA TEACHER'S REPORTS

KAZ, ELEMENTARY SCHOOL STUDENT

You know, we got our Weekly Reader newspaper—just as we did in our old schools. In one issue, they had a contest to depict scenes of WWII. So I sketched a battle scene; the bombs blowing up and the barbed wire and the trenches and the tanks. And I won! I was one of the students who won defense stamps. They published my name and address as one of the award winners!

A little later, I got a letter from a grammar school back east somewhere. This teacher was telling me that they were studying about the Wild-West and the cowboys and so she saw my address in Wyoming and figured I'd be able to provide them with some interesting stories about cowboys of Wyoming! [Kaz couldn't help laughing as he told this story] Little did she realize why I was there or where I came from!

So, I wrote back and said I'm from LA. and we're in this camp, we called it a relocation center, that was the proper term, Heart Mountain Relocation Center, and I'm sorry, I don't know anything about the cowboys of Wyoming. I know nothing about Wyoming.

Well, I never heard from that teacher again. I was thinking when they saw my address 29-1-D HMRC, that should have triggered something; that's a strange address, isn't it? But a lot of people didn't seem to know much about the camps or maybe they didn't put it together. A lot of people in the country didn't know anything about our evacuation.

Kaz Shiroyama interview with JFO 11/7/04

During the first school year, they went to class in barracks with no desks or supplies; workers built benches and tables to use until the new school was built.

NANCY MATSUMOTO

Grace Sachiki Hayami, known as Sach.

Soon after arriving at Heart Mountain, many college-aged prisoners launched efforts to get permission to leave camp, either to attend college in the Midwest, or to take jobs. My uncle Tosh, who had been forced to drop out of UCLA when the orders to evacuate came, left Heart Mountain in late 1943 to work at a boarding house on the north side of Chicago with some friends. He also enrolled at Illinois Tech, earning all of his tuition money through his job. He completed his sophomore year before being drafted into the army. My Auntie Terry, meanwhile left Heart Mountain later to take an office job in Chicago.

Stanley Hayami's sister, Sach started begging their parents to let her apply to a college on the same day that Stanley started his diary. Several of her friends had already left for Chicago, St Louis, and even New York. They were in college thanks to the National Japanese American Student Relocation Council, organized by the Quakers, who helped get many college age students into schools in the mid-west and east. Sach's parents were worried about their daughter being so far from the family and they didn't have money for tuition. Sach had friends with jobs taking care of children and cleaning houses during the day, and going to school at night. She thought that was a lot better than staying in camp and working in an office or the mess hall for $14 a month.

Stanley was truly surprised that she convinced them! 'Well I'll be darned,' he wrote in his diary, 'they've finally decided to let Sach go to college; it's to be Washington U in St. Louis...majoring in dress design.'

HAYAMI FAMILY PAPERS, JAPANESE AMERICAN NATIONAL MUSEUM

ALAN AND PETER, CODY BOYS

Alan

I remember seeing it the first time, yes. There were searchlights and barbed wire and when you drove to Powell that's what you saw. I don't remember going through the gate the first time....but I remember seeing it the first time, yes.

Peter

There was always a little trepidation, cause you had guard towers that looked like the movie version or Life magazine pictures of a concentration camp.

Alan

It was a tough time of total confusion for a kid because there were the "trustees" [trusted men and women from the camp] who came to town to work, there was the café with 'no Japs allowed' and then there were the gold stars in the windows, [meaning] someone had died in the service. And then, the Cody Enterprise would have another article about so-and-so killed in Germany or Japan and you knew 'they' were out there and you knew there had to be some reason for it—confusion, total confusion.

Peter

Well, our minister was a remarkable man named John McLaughlin. He took us out to there to run a church service. We were both acolytes.They held the services in the gymnasium. We set up an alter and we sat on either side of it and then when the services began, well, I remember that too was something of a revelation! They were doing exactly the same ritual we were saying the same words...doing all the same things. It was a good lesson.

HON. ALAN K. SIMPSON AND PETER K SIMPSON INTERVIEW WITH JFO 8/27/04

"My mom worked in Block 30, keeping the women's latrine clean...she was like a charwoman. That's how she earned her 16 dollars a month to buy us our clothes and ice skates. She must have saved for a lot of months to do that!"
-Kaz Shiroyama

NORM, ELEMENTARY SCHOOL STUDENT

That winter a new song was playing on the radio...White Christmas. I guess for the soldiers in the Pacific it was a song of longing, dreaming of a white Christmas and home. We didn't have to dream. It was right outside our doorsteps. But we didn't let that frozen wasteland go to waste. That winter the scouts helped with digging out the baseball field between the upper and lower block. Volunteers flooded the fields and they became ice skating rinks.

I remember I wrote to my sister in Chicago and told her they had made a pond. So the next thing I know, she sent me a pair of ice skates! I loved ice skating! That was just a real thrill! Now I used to always get kidded because of my ice skates. There are two types--the racing skates had a long nose to them and mine were figure skates and they had those little saw teeth on the front end. So kids always used to tease me about them. 'Normy's got figure skates!" But I was very proud of those figure skates and I loved ice skating.

Hon. Norman Mineta, Sec of Transportation
interview with JFO 10/14/04

STANLEY, HIGH SCHOOL STUDENT

Doggone it! Yesterday was my birthday and I didn't even know it. Today I was saying that it'll be two years more before I sign up for the draft, when Sach [his sister] says 'what do you mean you're seventeen now.' So I'm seventeen now. I don't feel like it. I mean I don't feel grown up like some people who are seventeen. Some are already out in the Pacific or someplace fighting.

Yesterday night I got a X'mas present from someone I don't even know... from a lady named Mrs. C.W. Evans who lives way over in Minominee, Michigan. I got the present via the Sunday School. Lot of other kids got presents, too. Walter, George and Tomo. Their presents came from all over the country. Walt's came from New York. Tomo's came from New Mexico. And George's came from Minnesota. Besides the presents everybody in the camp under nineteen gets a present whether they go to Sunday school or not. All the presents...were sent by the Presbyterian Union Church. I really think it was a fine gesture. I'm going to write to the lady as soon as I can.

...At about 7:00 o'clock I went to our mess hall Xmas party. It was lots of fun! We played some games, one of which I had to eat crackers and then whistle. I couldn't even eat one of the five crackers...After the games and entertainment Santa Claus came, much to the delight and happiness of the kids. George's little sister Sachie was so scared when she saw Santa that she cried.

Masoa and Tadao, and some other little kids went up to shake hands with Santa and get some candy and nuts from him. They looked as if they were in a trance. They came back holding up their package and looking intently at it. Then they showed them to everybody. Then they dragged out big boxes filled with presents for everybody.

I didn't expect much of this Xmas and instead I [had] about the most fun that I ever had.

STANLEY HAYAMI DIARY, DECEMBER 24 & 25, 1942, HAYAMI FAMILY
PAPERS, JAPANESE AMERICAN NATIONAL MUSEUM

NOB, JR. HIGH STUDENT

I recall a cold winter day. As I stared out the window ...what I saw was a mirror image of my barracks. There were 500 identical barracks in this camp and this mundane view was boring and provoked my mind to daydream. I thought of the good old days "back home" before incarceration. I thought about my home, friends, and classmates that I might never see again. I thought about the freedom to go anywhere at any time and do whatever I wanted to. I thought about eating my favorite foods instead of eating food I did not like but was forced to eat. I thought about picnics at the parks and beaches with my friends. I thought about the comfortable California climate. I thought about a bathroom with privacy, free from the eyes strangers. I missed all of these and much more. I yearned for them. Although ... I knew some of it was gone forever, I daydreamed about the future...Where will we be living? What will the government be doing with us? Are they going to ship us to Japan in exchange for Americans? I wonder what it will be like going to school on the 'outside.' I wonder how safe it is to live amongst a hostile public. I longed to live on the outside— living a normal life like other Americans. Is it possible?

NOBUYUKI SHIMOKOCHI INTERVIEW AND EMAILS WITH JFO 11/12/04

"As I stared out the window what I saw was a mirror image of my barracks. There were 500 identical barracks..."
- Nob Shimokochi

STANLEY, HIGH SCHOOL STUDENT

MY VIEWPOINT ON THE EVACUATION

Many people have written of the evacuation-have debates about it in heated discussions and have wondered how we feel. Well since I am one of those evacuated, although I may not be typical, but then who is? I will try to set down in writing what I think about it.

First of all, do I think that it was constitutional? No. I do not. We did not go thru the due processes of law. They didn't have any evidence. (It has been proven that there has been no sabotage done by the Japanese in Hawaii or the West Coast prior to or after the evacuation). However, it could have been legal, since the military doesn't have to go by the constitution in time of war.

Do I think racial prejudice was involved? Yes, I do. If it were not, how does one account for the fact that German and Italian aliens were not evacuated while Japanese American citizens as well as Japanese aliens were evacuated. Don't tell me we were the more dangerous. Germans and Italians can get closer to defense plants than Japanese can.

Do I think that it was worthwhile from the standpoint of the gov't? This is a very tough question as I don't know all the facts and what I say would be my opinion alone. My answer is that I don't believe that it was worthwhile to the gov't. Out of the 115,000 Japanese evacuated I doubt if there were any really dangerous ones. Instead of evacuating all of us — they should have kept an eye on us and just evacuated the worst of us. The evacuation also cost the gov't a tremendous amount of money and is continuing to do so. California faced a serious labor and food shortage due to the evacuation. Also many Nisei lost faith in America. Well now that I have gone over the whole Goddam situation what do I think in the final analysis?

I think the whole mess was unnecessary and a lot of trouble could have been avoided. However it did some good-that of breaking up the cliques. I personally will proceed to forget the whole, will try to become a greater man from having gone thru such experiences, keep my faith in America, and look forward to relocation and the future.

'Don't be afraid of opposition. Remember a kite rises against, not with the wind'. Hamilton W. Mabie

STANLEY HAYAMI DIARY, JUNE 1943

SEIICHI and TSUJI NAKO

Scouting began almost as soon as Heart Mountain opened and adults quickly realized the need for organized activities for young people. A husband and wife team, Seiichi and Tsuji Nako began making plans for scouting activities with a few other leaders.

In a temporary and unnatural kind of life as we have here, we wanted to provide something permanent for the young people. Scouting keeps them looking forward—gives them ambition—builds character.

HEART MOUNTAIN SENTINEL AUGUST 26, 1944

From the start, the Nakos had little in the way of equipment, facilities, trained leaders, or funds. About the only things they really had in abundance were enthusiasm and willingness. This was not new; the Nakos were active in scouting in Los Angeles before the war. Seiichi Nako was director of Troop 379, which had won national recognition in several music contests and raised funds from the Nikkei community to tour the country. Tsuji Nako had been associated with Girl Scouting for five years. They were determined to give the young people of Heart Mountain a rich scouting experience.

Now, after the shock of being confined in horse stables, these kids were faced with being imprisoned even farther from the homes they had known; for how long, no one could say. Mr. Nako was convinced that scouting would be more crucial than ever to keep the young people engaged. He spoke with the administration and with former scout leaders. They started with 150 former scouts— within a year 350 boys were scouts. Eventually, there were more than 750 boys participating in six Boy Scout troops and four Cub Scout packs. Joining the Scouts was one of the ways that young Japanese Americans declared themselves a part of the American mainstream.

50TH ANNIVERSARY, BSA TROOP 379 BOOKLET, AND HMS AUGUST 26, 1944

Left: Using the instruments brought along from Los Angeles Boy Scout Drum and Bugle Corps, Mr. Seiichi Nako organized and led a new Heart Mountain Boy Scout Drum and Bugle Corps. They marched and played for every major event.

ADMINISTRATOR NELSON

Find the attitude towards the camp getting worse in Cody and other places. Jack Richards [Cody Enterprise editor/photographer] who has given us so much cooperation has had to discontinue coming out to the project. Funny thing how people can change. A short time ago when they wanted these people to work in the fields they were fine people but now they are dirty yellow rats. I predicted that. I also predict that next spring when it's time to thin the beets again the feeling will be one of solicitation. Also, it hasn't been long since the merchants in Cody and Powell were proposing the operation of buses between Heart Mountain and the two towns so they could get some of the business. The Japanese people were fine people then, but now... Wonder if it would be the same. I doubt it.

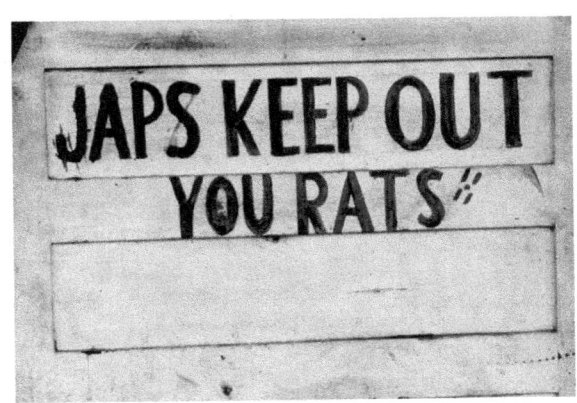

JOHN A. NELSON DIARY ENTRY, DECEMBER 26, 1942

LOUIS, ELEMENTARY SCHOOL, CODY BOY

Ten-year old Louis was pals with the Simpson brothers. His parents were Greek immigrants and ran the Mayflower Restaurant in Cody.

Adults from the Japanese camp came into town every Wednesday night to print the Japanese newspaper [The Heart Mountain Sentinel]; they printed it at the Cody Enterprise office. Well, their big thing every week would be to stop and eat at our restaurant, the Mayflower...it was two blocks from the newspaper office. All the other restaurants in town had signs in their windows saying they would not serve Japanese. We were the only one that did not. It didn't start out that way...at the very beginning. But, after a while, everybody had relatives who were in the Pacific and had friends and neighbors who were getting killed and then it became very anti-Japanese in Cody. I think we probably lost some customers—but it didn't make a bit of difference to my parents.

LOUIS KOUSOULOS INTERVIEW WITH JFO 8/27/04

A BRUTAL WINTER

Cartoon by Stanley Hayami, Tempo 1944,
Heart Mountain High School Yearbook

On January first, 10,767 people were imprisoned at Heart Mountain. In time as many as 14,000 men, women and children were held here in barracks with little or no insulation. That winter the mercury dropped to 28 Below Zero.

Still, they dreamed of the future.

I wonder how we will be traveling in the future. Perhaps we will have our own private autogiros and airplanes, which will be able to go to Europe in about a half a day. Perhaps twenty years from now the airplane and such will be obsolete, perhaps there will be entirely new traveling methods. Such as rocket ships. Maybe 50 years from now I'll be visiting the moon on afternoons. Maybe we'll be able to be radioed to Europe or Asia in person. Have a sending station which sends your molecules to a receiving station which assembles them in their proper places. Heck if this is impossible how about radio and television, I bet 20 years before they were invented nobody hardly even dreamed of them. Boy some fun I could have, just step into a sending booth, put some slugs into the machine and zip! I'm in Cairo, Egypt or Berlin, Germany (oops wrong number!) P.S. Well maybe I won't be able to get around that fast, but anyway after the war my biggest ambition is to travel around the world.

STANLEY HAYAMI DIARY, JANUARY 23, 1943

WRA LOYALTY QUESTIONNAIRE

The inmates had just about settled in, and the barracks were being insulated; school supplies were coming in and a real school was being built. That's when the government hit them with what they called "registration." It was really a loyalty questionnaire that everyone over the age of 17 had to sign. At first, it was just for men, but then they made it for everyone, Issei or Nisei, male or female. Two questions, in particular, aroused fear among both Issei and Nisei:

Question 27: Are you willing to serve in the armed forces of the United States on combat duty, or wherever ordered?

Did this mean that by signing the paper you were signing up to fight in the army? Men? Woman? Issei? Nisei?

And then there was Question 28: Will you swear unqualified allegiance to the United States of America and faithfully defend the United States from any and all attack by foreign or domestic forces, and forswear allegiance to the Japanese emperor, to any other foreign government power or organization?

NANCY MATSUMOTO

My father's parents were first-generation immigrants, or Issei, and were forbidden by law to become citizens of the USA. If they answered 'yes' to Question 28, foreswearing allegiance to the emperor, they would become people without a country. As for Question 27, most of them were close to 60 or older. Way too old to serve in the army. And they did not want their daughters in the army either.

The loyalty questionnaire divided my father's family. My paternal grandfather, outraged at his family's treatment at the hands of the U.S. government, and then on top of that to be asked to fight for the U.S. Army and renounce loyalty to his mother country, answered 'no-no,' and wanted his two oldest sons to do the same. His first son, my Uncle George (Atsushi) did but his brother Bill (Hideo) refused and answered 'yes-yes.' It caused a rift between father and son that lasted for years. But because my grandmother was pregnant, my grandfather ended up staying behind at Manzanar with three of their six children, while my Uncle George took my father David (Hiroshi), who was 14 at the time, and another under-age brother, Fred (Shigeru), with him to Tule Lake.

I regret never asking my father what that experience was like. He never spoke of camp or his time there to me and my siblings; we only heard the occasional offhand mention of it when he was with other family or friends. At such a young age, to be separated from his mother and placed in a notoriously rough and wild camp must have been traumatic for him.

Kura Morikichi and Family: Bottom row, L-F Kura, Morikichi, Fred (Shigeru); Middle row, Grace (Akiko) and Jim (Isao) ; Top row, Mae (Masako), George (Atsushi), and my father, David (Hiroshi)

YOSH, COLLEGE STUDENT

As a Nisei I really resented the question about the Emperor. I mean, how could we give up something we never had? If we answered 'yes' it would appear that we had been loyal to the Emperor at one time. We were American citizens by birth and as such owed no allegiance to the Emperor.

I made a rather naive statement, knowing they weren't going to accept the conditions any way. We were instructed that only a yes or no answer would be accepted. But, I put down a yes, provided my family is released from the camp and returned all their civil rights. I should have added "and restituted for their losses." All the time knowing it wouldn't make any difference anyway. Sure enough, they accepted the yes answer. Initially, I was just going to sign 'Yes, Yes' because that's how I honestly felt, but I thought surely in all fairness, they would release us first.

While their loyalty was being questioned, Yosh [far left] and other aspiring artists were turning out patriotic posters urging people to save tires, gas, and other essentials needed for the war effort.

That the questionnaire was an effort on the part of the government to try and determine whether we are trustworthy or not and to that extent I was willing to sign 'Yes, Yes.' Then I went to a few meetings and realized that just to be on the safe side, I better put a condition in there explaining my 'Yes' as far as military service is concerned—on the condition that the government returned our civil rights. I thought that was only reasonable.

YOSH KUROMIYA INTERVIEW WITH JFO 10/21/05

FRANK EMI

*I discussed the questionnaire with my brother Arthur
and decided I could not in good conscience sign 'yes'
to the loyalty document. I decided to answer both
questions with these words: 'Under the present
conditions and circumstances, I am unable to answer
these questions.' Knowing that others were also
confused about how to answer, we posted copies of my
reply on the mess room doors and other public places.
Many followed our lead.*

FRANK EMI INTERVIEW JFO 10/20/05

ADMINISTRATOR ROBERTSON, PROJECT DIRECTOR

*TO PEOPLE OF HEART MOUNTAIN: I feel that it is my duty to point out a number of
facts which have either been overlooked or intentionally disregarded by the leaders of
Heart Mountain. Heart Mountain has generally been regarded as a model relocation
center...Current registration for voluntary enlistment in the all-Nisei combat team has
cast a new reflection on Heart Mountain...*

*I would like to ask if the parents realize that a life-long stigma may be borne by their
children who fail to recognize and live up to their responsibility in the democratic
government and this may reflect upon your oft-mentioned desire to continue to live as
good citizens.*

*The administration has made every effort to help both the Issei and Nisei...to show
them the effect that their cooperation and non-cooperation will have on the whole
future of American-Japanese people who wish to make their future home in America.
No pains have been spared to get this problem thoroughly before the people in its full
significance.*

We believe that the great majority of the people of this center are either loyal United States citizens or friendly aliens...

Your government has asked outright that you express your loyalty. They have asked the alien to indicate his friendship... Your government has offered the citizen an opportunity to volunteer in the armed forces of the United States...

The response to these sentiments at Heart Mountain has been very, very disappointing. May I ask the citizen group how they expect to approach their government in asking concessions, whether it is restitution, reparation, or whatever you may ask, when you have more or less repudiated your government by failing to indicate a fair average of enlistment comparable to other relocation centers....

Project Director Guy Robertson

In view of the fact that you have not offered your wholehearted support to your government's program, you will be judged by the answer you have made...If you have reacted favorably, you will be considered favorably. If you have reacted unfavorably, you will, in all probability, have unfavorable consideration. Surely you understand that you cannot hope to force any issue with the government of the United States.

MEMO GUY ROBERTSON, PROJECT DIRECTOR, WRA PAPERS 5/5/44

On January 30th—just about the time the Loyalty Questionnaire was sprung on prisoners, the army decided the Nisei—men and women—were not enemy aliens, after all. So, they could serve in the war. Of course, that didn't include the Navy or the Air Corps— and no, not even the regular army. They wanted Nisei men to sign up for a segregated Regimental Combat Team, just for Japanese Americans. Nisei men who had tried to sign up immediately after Pearl Harbor were rejected in 1941 and classified as 4C and Enemy Aliens. Now, overnight they were declared 1-A, available for military service. It struck many inmates, like my grandfather and uncle, as ludicrous.

STAN, HIGH SCHOOL STUDENT

On January 30, 1943, the Sentinel announced the Nisei's new status.

Last Tuesday night I went to a meeting held by the army concerning the new order opening voluntary enlistment in the army. There were four men from the army altogether. A lieutenant, two sergeants and a Japanese American sergeant. They gave a lot of talks telling us how we would benefit if we volunteered. Said that the reason why they wanted to put us in a separate combat unit was for publicity.

A lot of people wanted to know if they could have some guarantees so that after the war was over, they wouldn't have their citizenship taken away, and the lands they own taken. They answered that we would be protected by the 14th amendment in the Constitution. Then one man says 'Well the 14th also is supposed to have kept us out of camp, what about that?' The

army answered by saying that in time of war the 14th and such do not hold and army has control and can do practically anything.

Then one man says, 'What the heck, are we going to get kicked out every time a war comes up?' Then the army man said that he agrees that a great injustice was done us when we were kicked out, but he says that the army has realized that what they did was probably wrong, and is now trying to help us to make up for it. He says that if we volunteer it'll do a lot to show our loyalty, and improve the relations and opinions of the American people toward us. It'll show that we are truly Americans, because we volunteered despite the kicking around that we got. On the other hand however he says if we all do not volunteer it'll be the other way around. Instead of improving our relations with the other Americans it would make it worse.

STANLEY HAYAMI DIARY, FEB. 12, 1943, HAYAMI FAMILY PAPERS JANM

TAK, HIGH SCHOOL STUDENT

I went to one of the meetings with a lot of questions of my own. Thanks to my long-term interest in planes and flying, my main question was could I join the Air Force? The answer was no. And the Navy was also out of bounds. I remember being shocked and thinking, that's not fair. So, I stood up in their group and I said, "I don't know about you guys, but since they're discriminating against us, even to the point of serving in the Armed Forces, I'm not going. It's not right.

TAKASHI HOSHIZAKI INTERVIEW WITH JFO 11/04/2004

TOYOO NITAKE

The most interesting part of their talk was for us to volunteer in the army to fight for our way of life—our community and our democracy and here we are in a concentration camp. The MPs were guarding the gate to keep us in and I wondered if they realize where they are! I felt sorry for them in that they had a job to do, say what they had to say, and I assumed they must be very embarrassed to do it. They never mentioned that they are in an American Concentration camp. I bet they were glad when it was over so they can get out of Heart Mountain. I felt they should have apologized for the government putting us in there but they talked as if they were in any other town USA.

TOYOO NITAKE LETTER TO MIKE MACKEY

The government got a handful of volunteers, but folks were so angry, one Nisei volunteer left in the dark of night to avoid being beaten up. His parents were shunned, and his brother was roughed up. His father didn't come to the mess hall for weeks after his son left for the army. A lot of the Issei men felt his father should have stopped him from going.

The official caption on this WRA photo says: "Selectees from Heart Mountain Relocation Center departing from the Powell Draft Board for pre-induction physical...at Fort Warren, Wyoming." Selectees? No, that was doublespeak for Volunteers.

Word got out that Norman Mineta's sister, Etsu was engaged to Mike Masaoka, a JACL leader who was coming to visit her. People were so furious with the JACL they threw rocks in the window of their barrack. At the time, the JACL was pushing the idea that the army should use suicide squads of Nisei soldiers to fight the enemy and keep their parents in the camps as hostages. Well, at least the army rejected that idea. Although there are plenty who say they treated their boys as fodder—put them in harm's way, where the odds were stacked against them. The head of the JACL, Mike Masaoka, pushed the idea of an all-Nisei battalion and when it was approved, he was the first one to volunteer for that segregated unit. But not many followed his example.

The Issei were angry that the government expected their children to leave their families inside the concentration camp while they go off to fight for the government that imprisoned them. The army expected 2,000 volunteers from Heart Mt. alone. They got 36 boys.

ADMINISTRATOR NELSON

Things didn't turn out quite as planned during the week on the army enlistment. The boys didn't grab it like the army thought they would... I can't blame them. They have been shunned, pushed around, called aliens, thrown out of their homes and bundled off to practically concentration camps. They aren't going to jump at the first chance that shows up to get out of here and be recognized as citizens until they are sure it is bona fide. I wish that some of the men in Congress and some of the men that set the policies back in Washington could spend some time on these projects. They would then get the real picture of the situation. They would learn first-hand how the Japanese feel about these things. As it is they just imagine that they know. They listen to rumors (scuttlebutt ...) and think that because someone lives within a hundred miles of one of the projects heard something it must be true.

JOHN A. NELSON DIARY ENTRY, FEBRUARY 14, 1943

NANCY MATSUMOTO

Strange thing is, with all the anger, the majority of Issei and Nisei signed 'yes-yes' to both loyalty questions. For young men like my Uncle George, his 'no-no' decision haunted him for the rest of his life. He and others like him were shipped to Tule Lake with the other 'disloyals' and the understanding that after the war they would be repatriated to Japan.

Kids like my father, a minor, had no say. They became no-no's, too. Even though they were American citizens, they had to go with their parents, or in my father's case, his older brother.

But, they weren't the only ones leaving Heart Mountain. Once the loyalty oaths were signed, the War Relocation Authority, the WRA, let many Nisei, like Sach and Frank Hayami leave. They were American-born citizens who were able to get jobs and attend midwestern and eastern colleges.

Nancy's Uncle George

JOY, HIGH SCHOOL STUDENT

Things were looking up in the high school...a new building was going up and it was going to have a huge gym and real classrooms with books! Two years ago, back home, we took things like that for granted--books, microscopes, typewriters, that kind of stuff. Not here.

Some of my friends urged me try out for George Igawa's jazz band's vocalist position. I had no experience, but fortunately they hired me (as a non-paid willing volunteer). What a release from boredom, from being in captivity. To sing so many wonderful songs with a big orchestra would have happened only in camp for me. We played at school dances.

The band consisted of about 11 to 14 band members plus the vocalists. That winter we were invited to play at dances in nearby towns to raise money for war bonds. It was fun getting out of the camp, except, at most of these places we didn't get fed. I guess they don't serve Japs.

Funny how we were expected to volunteer when they needed music or help harvesting the crop but the signs on stores in town still said: No Japs!

JOY TERAOKA E-MAILS AND CORRESPONDENCE 6/9/05-9/05

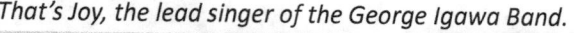

That's Joy, the lead singer of the George Igawa Band.

The George Igawa band often played for school dances in the new Heart Mountain High School gym. In fact, the high school and gym stirred up serious resentment in the local communities. That school inside a barbed wire fence had a gym that was a lot newer and bigger than any school gyms on the other side of the fence.

Heart Mountain High's school dance, March 17,1944, which must have been a St. Patrick's Day Dance. Like high schools everywhere, there were dances and proms in gyms decorated with streamers and a prom queen and king chosen to reign for the night.

Heart Mountain High's basketball teams didn't go out to play in the neighboring towns, but there were intermural games with visiting teams from Cody, Powell, and other nearby towns that came to Heart Mountain. Competitive sports were mostly for boys at the time, although the girls' basketball team of Heart Mountain and neighboring towns did play against each other. Heart Mountain and neighboring towns did play against each other.

A hotly contested basketball game between Heart Mountain and Powell High School girls teams; Heart Mountain girls were victorious, with the final score of 32 - 24.

CODY HIGH SCHOOL STUDENTS: LOUIS, FLOYD & BABE

Louis: There was no socializing before or after the game either...we went out there all suited up ... and we got on the bus or maybe we went in cars...We went out there and shot baskets for 5-10 minutes and then the game started...We played the game and then we left; we didn't shower out there and we left...it was pretty limited...it was just in and out.

Babe: I was a cheerleader. We'd go out there and cheer...they had their own cheerleaders and we always visited with them, socialize...like you always do with opposing teams' cheerleaders...always fun...Maybe girls are just more sociable than guys...also [the guys] are wanting to win – it's more about competition. It was not live or die for cheerleaders.

Floyd: They [meaning the Heart Mt players] were very small, of course...compared to our teams. I was 6'2" and their tallest man was probably 5'3'...or 5'4". I have this article, [Floyd showed me a clipping dated Dec 31, 1943, Heart Mt Sentinel.] Cody scored 31-10!

Cody High School's athletic teams were (and still are) called the Cody Broncs. The Bronc colors were Gold and Blue. The Pep Squad Cheerleaders wore solid blue slacks, a white blouse covered by a gold sweater with a large blue "C" on the front. No short skirts or bare tummies in those days. Most of us kids had nicknames, mine was "Fudd" like Elmer Fudd. Don't ask me why, I never did know.

Louis: It was kind of strange to be going out there, to tell you truth, because here in Cody there was a lot hostility toward those people out there...you know, they were those dirty Japs, that's what they were called, "dirty Japs" who bombed Pearl Harbor and killed a lot of boys over there—so, there was a lot of bad feelings in Cody about the Japanese. As I remember, they'd send one of their people into town to do some shopping for probably, I don't know, probably for 40-50 people. He'd have a list and he would be an elderly man, that posed no threat to anybody, you know what I mean? He wasn't a young husky guy or smart ass or something like that...he was a gentleman who spoke good English and he'd come around and do the shopping he could do in stores that would let him in. There were some with signs on the door. "No Japanese" or "No Japs" as they called them...as I remember, the majority of them had those signs.

FLOYD DOLCE, LOUIS KOUSOULOS INTERVIEW WITH JFO 08/27/04
BABE MARTOGLIO, INTERVIEW WITH JFO 07/25/06

Heart Mountain's Eagles lost badly to Cody High, but during the 43-44 basketball season, they won 10 out of 19 games, despite their lack of height. They showed plenty of fight as they faced off with Worland, Lovell, Thermopolis, Burlington, Powell, Deaver, Cowley, Byron, Red Lodge, and Cody.

REPERCUSSIONS

> ## 'Japs Petted and Feasted in U.S. While Americans in Nippon are Tortured'
>
> - Denver Post

ADMINISTRATOR NELSON

Looks like we are in for a storm. Many of the senators are demanding an investigation of the WRA. Seems that stories have been reaching to the effect that we are pampering the Japanese; that they don't have to work; that they have fine bathrooms, and that they are eating better than the other Americans.

John A. Nelson Diary Entry, January 17, 1943

On the heels of the unrest over the loyalty questionnaire and call for volunteers, the nation was outraged by news that the Japanese had executed three U.S. airmen who were captured a year earlier and held and tortured as prisoners of war. Those inside the WRA camps were as outraged as citizens all over the country.

BILL HOSOKAWA, Editor-in-Chief, *Heart Mountain Sentinel*

War, by definition, is inhuman. It's first objective is to kill, maim or otherwise incapacitate the enemy before he can do the same to you. It is a brutal and degrading business.

Perhaps it is ironical that man, unable to outlaw war, has sought to humanize it by international covenant. Those covenants...are a safeguard against barbarism...Japan by her own admission has broken that part of the covenat.

This act of unwarranted barbarities is condemned by all civilized people...Thousands of American soldiers of Japanese descent know that they may well face a similar or worse fate should they be captured. Those who volunteered recently made the decision with open eyes. Regardless of ancestry, they are Americans too, dedicating their lives to defend the principles, which collectively make up the American way of life.

Others would do well to remember that race is the only thing that a Tokyo Jap has in common with the Japanese American and his parents who repudiated their native land and decided 30 or 40 years ago to make their future with the United States.

HMS APRIL 24,1943

For teenagers, days were filled with school, ball games, dances, and clubs. But in the world beyond the barbed wire fence, a new surge of anger and resentment was growing. Renewed attacks in the press were directed at the Nikkei, charging that food was being hoarded at Heart Mountain, food not available to the public in general. One report claimed that 27,929 pounds of meat had been delivered to Heart Mountain, but neglected to write that the meat was to feed 10,000 people for more than eight days. In fact, meat was rationed for the Heart Mountaineers just as it was for civilians.

STAN, HIGH SCHOOL STUDENT

It seems that since the 'murder' of the Tokio bombers, who were captured by the Japanese, became known to the public sometime last week, public feeling seems to be pretty strong against us. Doggone it! Every time the Japs over there do something bad, we over here (we who have nothing to do with them over there-and who don't like them any more than anyone else) get it in the neck. Phooey!! STANLEY HAYAMI'S DIARY ENTRY, APRIL 29, 1943

In a column called Heart Mountain Glimpses, John Kitasako expressed his fears of repercussions:

We first heard about it-the execution of the American aviators-from a friend who had been listening to a radio broadcast. We hoped he heard wrong. When we tuned on our radio, we were gripped with that same nauseating sensation of horror that we had experienced right after Pearl Harbor.

Soon the whole camp was buzzing-condemning, cursing, deploring. Pearl Harbor was still fresh in everyone's mind. We knew that though we were 7,000 miles from the scene of that barbaric Tokyo execution, our lives and our future would be vitally affected. We would have to take the rap.

What we feared came to pass. Overnight, the pendulum of public sentiment swung against us. What had taken months of patient endeavor to establish friendly public relations was shattered in one fell sweep by the reverberation of the murderous volley of shots in Tokyo.

Camp morale has hit a new and miserable low. The resettlement program has suffered a devastating set-back. All we can do is to hope and to pray that the sentiment of the American public, once it has recovered from its awful shock, will differentiate between the American Japanese and the Tokyo Japanese. For there is a difference, a great difference. MAY 6, 1943 HMS

As the public reacted to the shocking news, Elmer Davis, Director of the United States Office of War Information spoke on a nation-wide radio broadcast:

There can be no peace with murderers. We must and will gain unconditional surrender...the salvation of our way of life rests on complete and irrevocable military victory....At Camp Shelby, in Mississippi there are three thousand American soldiers of Japanese ancestry; and they turned out yesterday and put the better part of a month's' pay into war bonds to show what they thought of this performance in Tokyo. Thousands of other Americans of Japanese blood, from Hawaii and relocation camps in the west, are now being inducted into the army—all of them tested and known for their loyalty to their country, and all of them just as eager to avenge this sort of behavior as are any other Americans. (April 23, 1943)

This affirmation of the patriotism of the Japanese Americans by a government official, distinguished between them and the enemy. But the general public was so angered by the murders that it needed a scapegoat, and the Nikkei became an easy target.

JAPS IN CAMPS GORGED WITH LUXURY FRUIT AND VEGETABLES

April 30, 1943

Bananas are very scarce in Denver. The few that the American Housewife can buy, at long intervals, are expensive...but at Heart Mountain.....the Jap guests of Uncle Sam don't have to worry about either scarcity or high price....because they are going to continue to get their bananas...and other delicacies that American Soldiers in Army camps in and around Denver never get, and that are very rarely obtainable by the American Family.

AMERICAN HERITAGE CENTER, UNIV. OF WYOMING

By Estelle Ishigo

Another article charged that the WRA had ordered 4,000 pounds of bananas for Heart Mountain, but the WRA replied ,"The total quantity of bananas received at Heart Mountain was sufficient to provide only one half of one banana for each person at the center and was used in a gelatin dessert."

BILL, JR. HIGH STUDENT

It's true, the communities around Heart Mountain asked why are we being pampered? Pampered because we had electric lights-the neighboring communities still had kerosene lamps, so they said we're being pampered. Yet coming from the city we think we're deprived because we only had one light bulb in a large room; it was so dark! It all depends where you're coming from. The neighboring communities were opposed to us having electricity because they didn't have it.

They said we had indoor plumbing, too. True, it was indoors, but you had to walk to it...no, it was not in the barrack. It was a community bathroom. That was one of the most embarrassing things in camp--doing your business next to strangers, all the commodes are just lined up. In the beginning people used to wait for darkness to do their business...but I think everyone else had the same idea, even at ten, eleven o'clock at night. We would be lined up and the showers, too were open like high school people or in the army...just a community thing. The worse part, especially if you woke up in the middle of night and you have to go! You had to put all your clothing on and go outside in the dead of winter and walk 100-300 feet away...and then come back—you're wide awake by then.

BILL SHISHIMA INTERVIEW WITH JFO 11/05/04

*Bill Shishima,
Troup 333*

STANLEY, HIGH SCHOOL STUDENT

January 3,1943. Man! It's so cold tonight that my hair froze as I was coming back from the shower.

Today I went to Sunday school... but it was hard getting there. It was so cold (20 degrees below zero) that I bundled up until I looked like an Eskimo. James Nakada and I ducked into each laundry house on the way up. However, as soon as I take a hundred steps my

Cartoon by Stanley Hayami, Tempo, Heart Mountain Yearbook 1944

eyelids eyelashes would have icicles on them. So, when I get to the laundry room I melt the icicles off and keep on going. Anyway, I finally got there. Hardly anyone was there.

STANLEY HAYAMI DIARY, JAN. 17,1943, HAYAMI FAMILY PAPERS, JANM

As the firestorm over waste and coddling continued, politicians called for congressional hearings. Once again, the cry went up to ship all the Issei back to Japan and to strip the Nisei of their American citizenship and send them packing with their parents.

On April 30th, the Denver Post ran an editorial that included these words...

WHEN THIS WAR IS OVER, EVERY JAP IN THIS COUNTRY SHOULD BE SENT BACK TO WHAT IS LEFT OF JAPAN, AND NO JAP SHOULD EVER AGAIN BE ALLOWED TO LAND IN THE UNITED STATES.

ADMINISTRATOR NELSON

Frankly, I believe it would be a good thing if Congress would investigate the centers. What they would see would surprise them, I am sure. They would find old men and women and little children and babies having to go half a block in weather 20 to 30 degrees below zero to the community bath house. They would see these same people going the same distance to the community mess hall, scrambling to their places over at rough picnic tables—the kind with the seat fastened on and requiring the individual to go into contortions in order to get both feet under the table.

They would see children of all ages being fed the same kind of food—some badly

prepared—as the adults. They would see the school kids attending school in makeshift rooms because we haven't got the school houses finished. And if some of the politicians have their way, they won't be finished. One thing Congress and the majority of citizens have forgotten or won't admit is the fact that most of the Japanese in the centers are citizens and that as citizens they are given certain rights by the Constitution and of these United States.

No, they would set aside the Constitution and condemn without benefit of trial approximately 80,000 citizens because they are descended from Japan. We can't profess to lead the way in preaching the gospel of freedom from slavery of the suppressed groups in the axis countries if we turn barbarians.

JOHN A. NELSON DIARY ENTRY, JANUARY 17, 1943

JOY, HIGH SCHOOL STUDENT

There was so much anger about the loyalty registration that Mr. Corbett, our school principal, doubted many kids would turn out to dedicate the new flagpole. But, no matter what they say about us outside, there is still a lot of patriotic feeling. Ted Fujioka, our student president, told the principal not to worry. I saved this clipping from The Heart Mountain Sentinel to remember the day:

DEDICATION OF NEW FLAGPOLE

The snow-laden, north wind swept over the little company standing before the tall new flagpole; the snow greyed their hair and clung in little wet patches to their coats as they stood shivering in the slush underfoot.

At the foot of the flagpole the Boy Scout drum and bugle corps played earnestly, bareheaded and in shirt sleeves, and the wind lifted the bugles' blare, the booming of the drums and the crashing of the cymbals, and flung the militant and stirring dissonance like thunder over the prairie. Presently, at a sharp command, two scouts marched front and center, the most beautiful of flags between them.

Their fingers were stiff with the cold, and for a moment they fumbled with the halyard. Then slowly, the flag climbed the pole. The snow had stopped. There was a tiny patch of blue above where the sky tried to break through the overcast, and the bugles sang out the clear notes of "To the Colors." Suddenly the wind caught the flag and it fluttered out, whipping proudly from the halyard, the white and red and blue rippling against the patch of sky.

That was how Heart Mountain's new flagpole in the administration area was dedicated Tuesday this week. To the bareheaded handful that stood in the slush to salute their flag, it wasn't just the cold that brought the tears to their eyes.

"FLAG SALUTE" HEART MOUNTAIN INTERNEES, 1942. PHOTOGRAPH BY HANSEL MIETH

MOVING ON

So many comings and goings. People leaving for jobs, colleges, the army; hundreds more who had signed No-No were leaving and would be segregated at Tule Lake. But the barracks did not stay empty for long. In April, families like Sutter's, who had signed Yes-Yes were arriving at Heart Mountain's Vocation Station. Weekly issues of the Heart Mountain Sentinel had columns of thanks and farewell messages.

THANK YOU

We wish to express our grateful thanks and appreciation to Heart Mountain residents for the many kind remembrances and send-off given James upon his departure for active service with the army.

Teruko Sunahara and family, 8-4-B

THANK YOU

To friends and residents, we wish to extend our grateful appreciation for the many kind remembrances and send-off given Toshiyuki, prior to his departure for active service with the army.

Mr. and Mrs. Tatsujiro Shintani, 29-15-A
Tatsusuke Shintani, grandfather

THANK YOU

We wish to take this means of expressing our sincere appreciation to friends and neighbors for the send-off given our son, Spencer, upon his departure for active service with the army.

Mr. and Mrs. Seimatsu Sato, 24-9-D

THANK YOU

We wish to take this opportunity to express our sincere thanks to friends and neighbors for the send-off given our son, Hideo, prior to his departure for active service with the army.

Mr. and Mrs. Wasaburo Tachibana, 30-19-CD

THANK YOU

I wish to take this means of expressing my sincere thanks to the doctors, hospital staff and friends for the care and consideration given me during my recent illness.

Fumiko Miyade, 17-7-B

FAREWELL-THANK YOU

We wish to take this means of expressing our appreciation to friends and neighbors for the many courtesies extended us during our residence in Heart Mountain. We have gone to Granada.

Mr. and Mrs. Ritaro Hifumi, 20-17-D

THANK YOU

We wish to express our grateful thanks and appreciation to Heart Mountain residents for the many kind remembrances and send-off given our son, Tom, upon his departure for active service with the army.

Mr. and Mrs. Ichitaro Okumura, 30-6-C

IN APPRECIATION

We wish to extend our deepest gratitude to friends for the many expressions of kindness and sympathy accorded us during our recent bereavement.

Mr. and Mrs. Kishiro Fujimitsu, cousins
Block 15 residents
Saga Kenjin

THANK YOU

For the many kind remembrances and send-off given our son, Hiromi, prior to his departure for service in the army, we wish to extend our sincere appreciation to friends, residents and administrative personnel.

Mr. and Mrs. Ichiro Shinji, 29-15-A

THANK YOU

For the many kind remembrances and send-off given me prior to my departure for service in the army, I wish to extend my sincere appreciation to friends, residents and administrative personnel.

Kay Fujishin, 1-15-E

THANK YOU

To friends and neighbors, especially Block 30, residents, may I take this means to extend my sincere thanks for the gifts and send-off given my son, Toshi, prior to his departure for active service with the army.

Mrs. Fude Mayeda, 30-3-D

FAREWELL—THANK YOU

To the clergy, with whom I had the pleasure of working with the past year, to all Buddhist members, friends and neighbors, may I take this means of expressing my appreciation for the courtesy extended me during my residence in Heart Mountain. I have relocated to Chicago, Ill.

Rev. Gyomei Kubose, 14-3-E

THANK YOU

For the gifts and send-off given Donald upon his departure for service with the army, we wish to extend our grateful thanks to our friends and neighbors.

Kiyo Takakura, wife, 30-22-C
Reiko and Donald Jr., children

IN APPRECIATION

We wish to express our deepest gratitude to friends, especially Block 2 residents, for the memorial services held for the late Lt. Kei Tanahashi, who was killed in action in Italy on July 4.

Joy Tanahashi, wife
Soji Tanahashi, father
Kin Tanahashi, mother
Yasaku Hirano, father-in-law
Chiye Hirano, mother-in-law
Kiyoshi Tanahashi, brother
Fusaye Tanahashi, sister-in-law
Masako Fujii and Hanako Cho, relatives
Boy Scout Troop 879
Block 2 residents

STAN, HIGH SCHOOL STUDENT

Sunday, August 1, 1943

Last Thursday Frank left for New York. When he shook my hand to say good-bye, I could hardly say anything because of the lump in my throat. Gosh it's queer. I argue and quarrel with him, but when it comes to where he leaves I feel kinda sad. Shig Iseri and Coya Iwamoto (Frank's good pals) Anson, Eddie, Margaret and Alice and Papa were there, too. Ma went to sewing so she wasn't there. Sach said she couldn't stand saying good-bye so she didn't go. Walt was working in the poster shop.

Aug 25, 1943

Cousin Eddie left for the Univ. of Cincinnati today.

August 31, 1943

Sach left for Chicago—It was windy— Sach had some tears in her eyes— though she tried hard to fight them back—don't blame her. James Yada left yesterday for River Forest, ILL.

STANLEY HAYAMI DIARY, JANM

Almost at once, Stanley and Sach began a regular correspondence.

Sept. 6, 1943

Dear Sach,

Frank wrote last week again. He moved again! His address is

FRANK HAYAMI (OBVIOUS isn't it), Room 267 23rd St. YMCA, 215 WEST 23rd St.,N.Y.,N.Y.

The room he has now is swell he says, good bed, which a maid cleans, a towel a day, a good desk & chair, closet, set of drawers, book case, good soft arm chair, floor lamp, and a telephone. Rent is $6.50 a week.

Frank went to a lot of radio concerns but they won't hire him unless he has a defense plant clearance. Some won't hire him, because of his lack of experience, but some have promised him a job if he can get his clearance.

In the meantime he went and got a job in a cafeteria carrying dishes, washing dishes, and mopping the floor. He works from 12:00 noon til 9:00 P.M. One thing he likes about the job is he can eat anything he wants. I suppose it's free though he didn't say so. (its free I just read were it says so. He also gets $21.00 a week and uniform. But subtracting taxes he ends up with about $18.00.)... Frank also says for you to come to New York... Lots of rooms and stenographers get $5.00 a day. Also, lots of schools....

Anson left last week for Boulder, Colorado. He's going to work as a dishwasher for about 3 months in the University. Well that's about all for now so—adios.

Your brother

Stan

NANCY MATSUMOTO

Nancy's mother, Lillian (Sumiye), at Heart Mountain.

My Uncle Tosh (Toshio) was among the first to leave, to work and attend Illinois Tech. Later, my Auntie Terry left camp and found a job in Chicago.

As more and more families left, those who remained did their best to keep life as normal as possible. My mom, who was 10 years old, remembers playing with a box of toys and dolls that her family's loyal Filipino employee had shipped to her in camp. There were movies; most were old, but better than nothing. In the spring, baseball season started up. There were teams of school-aged kids as well as older players. Adults kept busy with their jobs as well as craft classes like carving, knitting, tanka poetry writing (which my grandparents loved), growing bonsai plants, and watching the baseball games. That spring the gymnasium in the new school was finished. The new school wouldn't be ready till fall, but some of the scouts remember sneaking into the building early in the morning to play ball. A few weeks later the gym was used for high school graduation exercises.

TED FUJIOKA, HIGH SCHOOL GRADUATE

Just two days after graduation Ted Fujioka startled his father by saying that he had decided to volunteer for the Army. According to his mother:

He explained that his decision was the result of no sudden impulse. He had been weighing the matter for weeks and had concluded that it was his 'sacred duty to his country and his people'. Although his father was startled, he spoke calmly... 'All right son if you are sure that it's what you want to do. This is your country; you are a citizen. But before you make up your mind finally, you should seek the counsel of your older brothers. When you have done so, come and talk to me again.' Ted talked to them. They agreed that he should volunteer since he felt the way he did. When he approached his father again, his father told him 'to go ahead and to be a good soldier.'

Not long after graduation, when Ted went to Cheyenne for his physical, he was asked if he wanted to enter active duty immediately. He said that he did and wired his folks that he would not be back.

COMMUNITY ANALYSIS SECTION, DEC. 8 1944, LETTER OF CONDOLENCE, NARA CONVERSATION WITH MRS. FUJIOKA WHEN LETTER WAS PRESENTED.

IKE, HIGH SCHOOL STUDENT

With help from my dad, we turned the space under our barrack into a darkroom where we developed photographs. Cameras had been considered contraband, but once Nisei soldiers came to visit on leave cameras began to show up inside the camp. "We used to develop our films and print photos at night because it was totally dark. Our father dug it out. It measured about 4x4 in size and about 4' deep. We cut a hole in the wooden floor with a "trap door" and a hinged entry from inside the barrack. It was hard work digging this out by hand. One time a friend came in and was walking toward me and didn't notice the trap door. Yes, he fell in! Fortunately he didn't get hurt.

Ike's photo with the bass drum was produced in the dark room built under their barrack. It was Mike who became interested in photography in camp and became an industrial photographer and teacher of photography years later.

IKE HATCHIMONJI INTERVIEW WITH JFO 11/04/04

JOY, HIGH SCHOOL STUDENT

In late August, my father got a job and we got clearance to leave. We walked outside of the gates of confinement forever and went to Salt Lake City where I attended East High. Two months later we shoved off to Denver; and three months after that we stepped into the hub of the nation, Washington, D.C. In the capital city I went to Calvin Coolidge High for the last part of my senior year. Though Heart Mountain High School has many fond memories for me, as we were its creators, I was thankful to have been one of the lucky people who graduated without the confines of restrictive fences, sentries, and an abnormal environment.

JOY TAKESHITA TERAOKA COLLEGE PAPER, 1/28/47

SACH, COLLEGE AGE STUDENT

Chicago, Illinois September 24, 1943

Dear Mom, Pop, Stan, and Walt----

I hope you are all well and happy. I am well and not sad but not happy either. I feel that I really work for this $4 a week that I get.

Mrs. and Dr. G. arranged a ride for me in the morning in a Hospital car that goes downtown every morning. This comes right to our door ... very convenient for me when it begins to snow, (and I save 50 cents a week on bus fare) but now that I leave a half hour later, I have to clean bathtubs, washstands, and toilets every morning in the two bathrooms upstairs in addition to the beds I make... Friday night, I had to defrost the refrigerator and wash it out with soap and mop the kitchen floor after I do the dishes. Tomorrow is the hard day. Every Saturday I have to dust everything in the whole house, wash off finger marks from the woodwork, vacuum every room and the draperies. Boy, oh, boy. Vacuuming draperies makes me want to cuss because it's sure hard to do. Saturday starts off the same as other days at 6:50 a.m. when I start making breakfast and it continues all day until after supper dishes which is about 8:30 p.m. Sunday mornings I make coffee at 6:50 a.m. Then the whole family goes to church around 9:00 and come home to have breakfast---a good heavy one around. 10:30. They leave the little two-year-old boy with me. He cries and cries at the beginning, but pretty soon he stops. So far he and the 8 year old girl have been pretty nice kids, but the 5-year-old girl...a nervous, underweight crybaby is a bit difficult at times. Anyway, to get back to Sundays, I am finished around 12 o'clock and have the rest of the day off. My first Sunday here I said I was going to study downstairs so Dr. and Mrs. G. went out and asked me to wash the dishes. I don't think that was fair, do you?

I got your nice letter, Pop. Thanks for the $10—I'll try not to ask for any more 'cuz I know you need it just as much as I. I'm trying to get along on the $4 I earn and just *pay tuition out of my savings. The school has begun to be more interesting, but we are not yet confident that it is the best place to be.*

Goom bye for now. [goom-bye was slang for good-bye]

Love, Sach

STAN, HIGH SCHOOL STUDENT

Oct. 22, 1943

Dear Sach,

Too bad you lost your job, but I guess you didn't like it much anyhow.

I'm going to send this letter by airmail tomorrow so everything will be fresher. Otherwise the news is stale by the time it gets to you...I didn't write much this and last week was because I had so much studying to do for the six-week tests...I got an A in Solid Geom. an A in Physics, an A in Art, and got a (sniff) B in English...

Frank hasn't written us for about 2 weeks now so I don't know how he is. We get worried when someone doesn't write so be sure and write when you get time.

Don't worry too much and don't get sick or nuthin'

Grace "Sach" Hayami.

The letter continues with Stanley quoting his father:

Don't worry 'bout jobu and if you need money I send it. Don't get any more domestic jobs. Best way is to try get steady part-time office job. Put advertisement in Chicago Tribune for job.

Eat plenty and don't worry when you lose jobu.

'Nother thing Papa wants to know is 'bout four blocks you walk from work to streetcar line after ten o'clock. Is four blocks busy and lighted or dark and lonely. If dark and lonely quit right away! Did you get tennis racket. I will write more Monday. If things go wring, best thing, take easy for 1 or 2 months without worrying about money or anything and take time and find good part time jobu for after school.

Switching to his own voice, Stanley wrote:

Fooey—Pa talked a little too much now I guess I'll write a little more so's I won't waste any paper. Well, what shall I scribble about...The time is now 20 min. to 10 P.M. Pop is already in bed. Lights are off, but Walts got the radio still on. Pa already "Ahemed" at him once.

Mom dreamed about you last Sunday night—she said you looked very tired. Are you? I suppose Ma has television dreams.

How is art school. Is it hard or is it easy.

I'm learning about watercolor here. My technic up to now and including now has been lousy. I'm learning how to put on the color with that "fresh" look and how to put on good looking skys...It seems that the more I learn about art, the more I see how little I know about it.

Well that's about all for now.

Papa, Naoichi Hayami

Stanley Hayami

HAYAMI FAMILY PAPERS, JANM

CHIZUKO, JR HIGH SCHOOL STUDENT

My parents were quite embittered by the incarceration and so they decided to return to Japan with my mother giving up her citizenship. One of the reasons for this was because of a loyalty oath they were forced to answer. I was too young to sign one. Looking back on it now, I am outraged at the cruelty of a government which asked people to sign a loyalty oath after putting us into concentration camps. It ripped families apart, set neighbor against neighbor, and was the cause of much anguish.

I did not understand my parents' feelings at the time so I fought them over the decision. I was dead set against going to a country I had never seen and did not consider a homeland. The alienation was so complete I did not speak to my parents for what seemed like months. I felt remote and separate from parents, family, peers, the society around me...

I have grown up with great mixed feelings about my heritage. For a long time, I had a dislike for things Japanese and for many Japanese Americans. Call it a projection of a certain self-hate and discomfort. I feel that the camp experience alienated me from my people. I turned my anger against them rather than the government...

For many years, I had put the camp experience out of my mind. It was as though a shroud-like covering had been put over the whole thing and so it remained repressed. My father and I never talked about it and only vague generalities were expressed when the topic came up. I got so I could talk about it quite objectively but with a great deal of distance.

The emotional content was missing. It was avoidance, a refusal to confront the pain of the experience. Also, it was a way of controlling a great mass of anger which was so concealed I wasn't even aware of it. Now, in thinking about it, I am always brought to the point of tears. Beyond the pain and anger is, I believe, a fear which has kept me silent...

With the passage of time, I feel more able to confront my history. I am impressed by the efforts of the Jewish community to commemorate the holocaust. In books, novels, dramas, TV shows, and other educational programs, those horrendous events are kept alive in our memories and coming generations will have access to them. We must make sure that coming generations of Americans also know about what happened to us.

TESTIMONY OF CHIZUKO OMORI, SEATTLE, SEPTEMBER 9, 1981

SUTTER, HIGH SCHOOL STUDENT

We were in Tule Lake Relocation Camp, near the California Oregon border when my dad got this paper and I asked what is this about? And he said it's a loyalty paper and I remember saying, "Well, we're Americans." But he said it's for the parents, only parents have to sign it. He went around to other people who didn't know what to do. Some were very upset. But he signed it. 'That's it, we're leaving,' he said.

I don't know when we learned that we were being sent to Wyoming. I just remember that most of my friends were going to Camp Amache in Colorado and I didn't know anyone at Heart Mountain.

One very close family from Sacramento, the Ota family – their son was the valedictorian in our high school; he was just starting college when the war broke out. He joined the 442nd and he died at the landing in Italy—it was very quick and he was one of the first to volunteer in '43. Anyway, his family did not want to sign the papers. People thought if they didn't sign they were in limbo, but if you didn't sign it was the same as saying no! That family ended up being sent to Japan.

SUTTER KAJITA TELEPHONE INTERVIEW WITH JFO 3/14/05

NORM, ELEMENTARY SCHOOL STUDENT

That fall the scout leaders invited the scouts from outside the camp to come in. Most people [outside] thought of this camp being for Japanese Prisoners of War. So when the invitation went out for the scouts to come in for a jamboree in the camp, they all thought I'm not going to go in there! They're a bunch of POW's so why should I go in there? So, someone explained—'Say these are a bunch of Boy Scouts of America. They read the same manuals you do; they wear the same uniforms you do; they go after the same merit badges that you do.' I guess over a period of time that message finally sunk in. The Boys Scouts from Powell and Deaver didn't come, but scouts from Cody came. So that's when we all got together.

I think to have these folks coming in was really something that everybody welcomed. It was fun. Essentially from, let's say May of 1942— except for MPs or people associated with the camps we really had not seen any Caucasians our own age. So, this was sort of fun to have kids of our own age coming into the camp. This was really welcome.

HON. NORMAN MINETA, SEC OF TRANSPORTATION INTERVIEW WITH JFO 10/14/04

ALAN AND PETE, CODY BOY SCOUTS

Peter

Our scout master was Glenn Livingston and he just said we're going out to the Japanese camp...they called it then the 'Jap Camp.' But I don't think he called it that. He said I've contacted your parents and those of you who can go I want you to just remember this—they take the same oath that you and I take. So, we're going to go out there for the jamboree.

Alan

I'm sure there were some who said, 'Oh no!' You know, their family member had been killed in the war and they said 'Stuff it!' I remember a sign downtown that said, "My son was killed in the war and no Japs allowed in here."

Peter

Our parents thought we should do it. They said tell us about the conditions.

Alan

Did we think the people behind the barbed wire were our enemies? Well, they were, because we were told that they had taken them from the coast and put them behind barbed wire. So, suddenly, 11,000 people are out here and everybody said if they ever got out they'd wipe out Powell. There were only 2500 over there. And Cody only had 3,000. So, by God, they better keep watch on them out there. They were pretty bad people! And then you go see them and all there was were grandmothers and guys over 45 and kids our age; all the younger guys were in the army.

Alan and Peter Simpson

Peter

They spoke perfect English. I think I was surprised...they spoke the same slang.

Alan

They spoke the same junk we did...that was the big revelation.

Peter

I think we ate sloppy joes...hamburgers...all the scouts...that we were all eating the same chow, and playing games and doing merit badges...

Alan

Telling dirty jokes..

Peter

I was surprised they knew things we knew.

Alan

At that field day, I remember a little kid, Norman Mineta...and we talked about merit badges we had earned, not many. He remembers the knot tying thing and a tent with water that ran off on some other guys and I said Norm you made that up...

Hon. Alan K. Simpson and Peter K. Simpson interview with JFO 8/27/04

NORM, ELEMENTARY SCHOOL STUDENT

[But Norm insists he was not making anything up...]

So, it turned out Alan and I were paired off to put up a pup tent. Whenever you have a pup tent...what you have to do is to build a moat to protect the tent in case it rains. So we built our moat. Then, Alan said, "There's a kid from my troop in the tent just below us here. Would you mind if we make the water--if it rains--go that way?"

So, I figured, it's no skin off my nose. So, I said, 'Sure.' So we cut our moat very nicely and then we cut where the water would exit , so it would drain this way. And later that afternoon, as luck would have it, it really rained. Our moat worked perfectly, and the water drained his way and pretty soon the tent pegs down there pulled and the tent came down and Alan is sitting here going, "he-he-he!" I used to tell people I knew Alan when he had hair and he was roly-poly. He was really – I would say fat. I always tell people he was as ornery then as he is today.

Hon. Norman Mineta, Sec of Transportation interview with JFO, 10/14/04

KAZ, JR. HIGH STUDENT

Donald Yamamoto won the 'knot-tying' contest ...that's because he organized those strips of rope in such a way... practicing...all these things...he was doing it quietly on his own.... and he said first of all I got the twelve ('cause you have to tie 12 knots). And he said for some of the knots he needed stiff rope and for some he needed softie rope and he had planned it all and then he figured out a way to tie that was quicker than the way we had learned to do it—in the boy scout handbook. I could still tie those knots today...he taught me how to do it. So, he won the rope tying contest when we had the Boy Scout jamboree. We would have these contests and we also won the signaling contest...the other troops were using the semaphore flags...and the Morse code—'did dat dat' and all that. But we learned to communicate with the deaf hands mute signals and we were real fast with our fingers whereas the flags took time to signal every letter. So, we won that and we won the marching contest

Kaz Shiroyama interviedw with JFO 11/7/04

BILL SHISHIMA, JUNIOR HIGH SCHOOL STUDENT

One of the spectacular events of the field day was the pie eating contest. I remember it...I won!

JOY, HIGH SCHOOL STUDENT

I hadn't heard from Ted for a while. Then in The Eagle, our student newspaper, I was happy to read a long letter from Private Ted Fujioka, who seemed to love army life. He wrote:

It's a wonderful Sunday morning —the weather is perfect, the sky is blue and the sun is shining. The radio is playing soft religious music and there's a peaceful, quiet atmosphere throughout our camp. I can barely hear the KPs scrubbing pots and pans at the mess hall, and the occasional slamming of a door. It's hard to believe that all these men stationed at such a seemingly peaceful place are training for war, becoming accustomed to the handling of deadly weapons. There seems no rhyme nor reason to all this killing.

Private First Class Ted Fujioka

Yesterday was quite an experience for me as I participated in the regimental parade. We passed in review for the top ranking officers of our unit, dressed in our best khakis and bearing rifles, the colors, and our company standards. It was awe inspiring, just like the reviews of crack troops, that one sees in the movies... The Stars and Stripes stood out against the white sand, clear blue sky, evergreens mingled with autumn colors, and the row on row of neatly-clad soldiers. It's funny how a choking feeling of pride swells up inside of you as you watch young soldiers marching past the reviewing stand in perfect step to the music of our band. As our group passed the stand and we faced right, I couldn't help smiling a little with joy, with pride for our regiment is a crack outfit if ever there was one. You couldn't find better soldiers any place. I'll never forget the thrill of my first parade!

Letters from home are just about the best thing a soldier can possibly get. Just the knowledge that the ones at home are thinking of you helps so very much... You know, I consider myself one of the luckiest fellows in the world. I have everything to fight for. I have the finest parents a fellow could hope for, brothers and sisters who care as well, and the nicest girlfriend waiting for me. It gives a fellow courage, faith and hope. I suppose that a fellow who volunteers for a combat team isn't supposed to think of coming back – but I can't help praying that I will be able to return to all that I love after the war.

As ever, Ted

THE EAGLE, OCTOBER 26, 1943

BABE, CODY HIGH SCHOOL STUDENT

Our theme for the Pep Squad dance was White Christmas. Of course, that was a popular new song from the movie Holiday Inn. We went up to cut fresh trees so we could flock them all white for the dance. One of my friend's father had a big truck and a Japanese man working for him. So, he sent his driver with us to help us; to drive the truck and help us load the trees. I think his name was Tojo. He was from Heart Mountain. Anyway, on the way home, there was a place called the Green Lantern and they always had homemade ice cream and we never went by there without stopping and getting some ice cream cones. And the door—the screen door was pushed open so we couldn't see the sign that said, 'NO JAPANESE ALLOWED.' So we went in there and the man who owned the place started after this Japanese guy with a knife— because he had lost a son in the South Pacific. He was very emotional ... and all of us tried to stop him and we ran out—very definitely without our ice cream cones!

BABE MARTOGLIO INTERVIEW WITH JFO 07/25/06

A NEW STATUS
DEFENDING THE COUNTRY
DEFENDING THE CONSTITUTION

VOL. III, No. 4   Heart Mountain, Wyoming   Saturday, January 22, 1944   2 Cents Within City 5 Cents Elsewhere

Selective Service Opens for Nisei

YOSH, COLLEGE AGE STUDENT

It was right after the New Year, Jan. 22, 1944, to be exact, when the headline in our school paper announced: 'Selective Service Re-Opened to Nisei.' In other words, the government wasn't asking for volunteers anymore. We were about to be drafted out of camp, leaving our families behind barbed wire while we were expected to serve the same country that imprisoned us.

Let me tell you, that set off fireworks. A week later there was a big public meeting. In fact, there were meetings almost every night of the Fair Play Committee. More than 200 Heart Mountaineers joined together to protest. How could the government take away their civil liberties and then turnaround and draft them, demanding that they make the ultimate sacrifice for the country that took away their rights?

Even after the first meeting I always went alone and I never discussed the issue with anyone else. I liked what I heard from the leaders. I admired Kiyoshi Okamoto, who was way too old to be drafted, but who seemed to know so much about the Constitution. Frank Emi, another of the leaders and Paul Nakadate both had families, so they were not in line to be drafted. Yet, they were saying out-loud things that I had been thinking and feeling. They were not talking about themselves, but the rights of those who were being drafted. They were not pro-Japanese; these were men who believed in the Constitution of the United States and the rights of citizens.

YOSH KUROMIYA INTERVIEW WITH JFO, 10/21/05

SAM, COLLEGE AGE STUDENT

I was one of about 30 young men who did get on the first bus that took us for pre- induction physicals at Fort Warren in Cheyenne, the capital of Wyoming... the physicians giving the exams were Navy doctors who had been at Pearl Harbor on December 7th and they were strongly opposed the idea of admitting Japanese Americans into the military. They rejected all the Nisei except me. I don't know why exactly, but I was the first and the only one admitted that day.

When I got back to Heart Mountain, even after I passed the physical, my dad took me to the Fair Play Committee meeting, He wanted me to listen to what they were saying. I listened but decided to go anyway. My dad was not unhappy with my choice. In fact, he showed me a card from WWI, when he was classified as 1-A and was to be inducted into the U.S. Army; but the war ended before he was inducted. He said he would pray that the war would be over before I had to go overseas....from that night on, I was comforted in knowing...my father left the decision to me and he was proud of the decision I had reached...later, he and my family had to endure the taunting...of those who did not share my views.

SAM FUJISHIN TO MIKE MACKEY

WALT, HIGH SCHOOL STUDENT

Stan told me he was going to meet with our cousin Alice's husband, Paul Nakadate, one of the leaders of the Fair Play Committee. When he came back from that meeting he told me, 'I kind of agree with them but there are two sides to this and I have decided to go'.

Walt Hayami interview with JFO 11/04/2004

Late in March they took the young recruits to Denver where there were Colorado doctors who were not opposed to drafting Nisei soldiers. Tempers heated up as more draft notices arrived. That's when the Fair Play Committee (FPC) issued several powerful manifestos. This final one was perhaps, the strongest.

We, the members of the FPC are not afraid to go war – – we are not afraid to risk our lives for our country. We would gladly sacrifice our lives to protect and uphold the principles and ideals of our country as set forth in the Constitution and the Bill of Rights, for on its inviolability depends the freedom, liberty, justice, and protection of all people including Japanese Americans and all other minority groups. But have we been given such freedom, such liberty, such justice, such protection?

NO!! Without any hearings, without due process of law as guaranteed by the Constitution and Bill of Rights, without any charges filed against us, without any evidence of wrongdoing on our part, one hundred and ten thousand innocent people were kicked out of their homes, literally uprooted from where they have lived for the greater part of their life, and herded like dangerous criminals into concentration camps with barbed wire fences and military police guarding it, AND THEN, WITHOUT RECTIFICATION OF THE INJUSTICES COMMITTED AGAINST US NOR WITHOUT RESTORATION OF OUR RIGHTS AS GUARANTEED BY THE CONSTITUTION, WE ARE ORDERED TO JOIN THE ARMY THRU DISCRIMINATORY PROCEDURES INTO A SEGREGATED COMBAT UNIT! Is that the American way? NO! The FPC believes that unless such actions are opposed NOW, and steps taken to remedy such injustices and discriminations IMMEDIATELY, the future of all minorities and the future of this democratic nation is in danger.

Thus, the members of the FPC unanimously decided...that until we are restored all our rights, all discriminatory features of the Selective Service abolished, and measures are taken to remedy the past injustices...we feel that the present program of drafting us from this concentration camp is unjust, unconstitutional, and against all principles of civilized usage. Therefore, WE MEMBERS OF THE FAIR PLAY COMMITTEE HEREBY REFUSE TO GO TO THE PHYSICAL EXAMINATION OR TO THE INDUCTION IF OR WHEN WE ARE CALLED IN ORDER TO CONTEST THE ISSUE..."

FAIR PLAY COMMITTEE BULLETIN #3

YOSH, COLLEGE AGE STUDENT / RESISTER

During the next days and weeks several of the guys refused to report for their pre-induction physicals. My notice came the day before St. Patrick's Day. I was insulted by the notion that I should be asked to fight for principles on foreign land that I was denied at home. I talked to my father about this, but he left the whole issue in my hands. He wouldn't give me any hints even as to what he would have done, but I think he would have done exactly the same thing and I was prepared to take the consequences.

At a Fair Play meeting, the mess hall jammed packed, we were asked for a show of hands as to how many of us had received our notices. I stood up and said I was to report to Powell on the 23rd of March, but I would not do so. The crowd cheered so loudly the windows rattled!

But not everyone in my life approved of what I was doing! As the day for my exam came closer my mother asked, 'Why can't you just go along like everybody else? Don't make waves! Don't draw attention to yourself!'

My father came right out and said, it's my decision, and whatever I decide he'll go along with, because he can understand the pluses and minuses either way. My parents weren't the problem, it was my sister-in-law. She was the real problem.

When she heard about it, what my intentions were, she stopped me outside and she had her little Kiyoshi, he was just short of one year old and she told me that she thought it was shameful what I was doing and how that would affect Kiyoshi's life—to have an uncle who's an ex-con—because even then we were pretty sure that our chances were pretty slim. We had to assume that we are going to end up in prison! She was pretty vehement about that, as a matter of fact, she went so far as to say that if she knew that her husband's brother was such a coward, she never would have married him.

I was hurt by what she said, but not enough to change my mind.

YOSH KUROMIYA INTERVIEW WITH JFO 10/21/05

On March 25th the Heart Mountain Sentinel reported that "residents were expecting the imminent serving of warrants on 12 local Nisei charging failure to report for selective service pre-induction physicals." In other words, they would soon be arrested.

MITS, RESISTER

I had three brothers who served in the army. But I refused. Why was I a Resister?

The main reason was...my constitutional rights were denied me when I needed them the most.

Laws under the Constitution, which were written to protect all American citizens, were flagrantly violated to put innocent Nisei and their parents into concentration camps. We were denied the writ of habeas corpus, the right of a trial to prove our innocence. Despite all of these constitutional violations, I was willing to be drafted. But in return, I wanted my constitutional rights as a free American first.

I said that if a person is going to fight for freedom and democracy, shouldn't he be enjoying the same rights he is entrusted to defend? I just couldn't understand why I was asked to fight tyranny overseas when my family and relatives were prisoners in a concentration camp. Most of the Nisei knew that we were herded into a concentration camp because of racial prejudice and not from military necessity.

MITSURU "MITS" KOSHIYAMA TO MIKE MACKEY

Mits later recalled that his ideas were shaped in 7th Grade when bullies in the school yard called him "Jap" and other racial slurs and he ended up in detention for defending himself. But the teacher in detention made him read the Constitution and wanted him to understand it was there to protect all citizens, to protect their rights.

And Mits was not the only one questioning the government's actions. In March of '44, 922 Nisei and 1,208 Issei parents signed petitions stating they were in accord with Nisei being inducted —but not segregated. They wanted to serve side by side with other Americans in all branches of the military. They wanted full restoration of their civil rights under the Constitution with the same treatment as other Americans. They wanted their families to be allowed to return to their homes and businesses and that the government abolish propaganda against Japanese living in the United States. Despite their willingness to fight, the petitions were ignored.

Looking less than sure of himself, that's Mits in courtroom; he's the one in the middle looking down.

YOSH, COLLEGE AGE STUDENT / RESISTER

On March 25th the U.S. Marshals arrested 12 men who failed to show up for their induction physicals. During the next days 25 more were arrested. The day they came for me they didn't make a show of it—they did their job. The FBI agent and a federal marshal drove right up to the front of the barrack and knocked on the door. My mother was there. I asked if I could just go to the restroom before we go. So, I went out the back door of the washroom and went to say goodbye to my girlfriend...by the time I got back my mother was almost in tears...because the agents were getting a little nervous.

Later on, I wished I had gone to the bathroom—it was a long drive. There were about 5 or 6 guys in the car. They took us to Cody to fingerprint us. Then, they took us all the way around to Powell, Lovell, Sheridan, and eventually to Cheyenne. But it was too full there, so they came across to Rawlins. I remember going through the Wind River Canyon to Thermopolis. If you went through there I guarantee you would not forget it! It has sheer cliffs on both sides--the highway on one side and the river on the other side. It was beautiful—with patterns on the rock. It was fantastic, almost like going through a tunnel.

We were just like teen-agers. I was 20 at that time. We were a pretty young bunch. They put us in the jail there in Rawlins... a small community jail but it was clean. We were the only inmates so they let us have the run of the whole area. We didn't look dangerous. The only time we went into the cells was to sleep in the bunks.

Later we were taken to the overcrowded, old, and dark Laramie County jail in Cheyenne that was built to accommodate half the number of men crammed into the musty cells. I had a mattress and ratty old blanket that reeked of vomit and urine. We were there more than 2 months. Guys had to sleep on the dirty floor and we had to step over others to go to the toilet. The food was inedible.

YOSH KUROMIYA INTERVIEW WITH JFO 10/21/05

Articles from the Heart Mountain Sentinel and the JACL's newspaper the Pacific Citizen contained vicious attacks on the resisters calling them cowards, draft dodgers, and traitors. Many considered the resisters and their families an embarrassment and their families were shunned. In fact, one of the resister's mothers was so distraught that she took her own life. After reading his mail, Tak wrote in his journal, "We received a 'Sentinel' today and we all read it. Judging by it, they must be drafting those guys in camp awfully fast. I guess they want them in the army before our trial ends."

JACK, RESISTER

By late March there were 63 Resisters scattered in jails all over Wyoming.

Tak in the courtroom, the tall one, center of the picture.

We had bedbugs and someone told me that the crunchy parts of the oatmeal were cockroaches' legs. Life in the Cheyenne jail made Heart Mountain seem like a paradise lost. Most of all, I had to admit that I missed my family. In April, we had two visitors from camp who tried to convince us to change our ways and we could get out of jail. They said we were damaging the image of our people. But I told them if I didn't protest the way we were being treated, I would be just as responsible as those who made the decision to put me in prison. A citizen who will accept bad government without protest is a bad citizen!

During this era President Roosevelt said many, many times that it's the duty of the citizens to preserve democracy. I often questioned myself, "What citizens? What democracy?" At that time, we were part-time citizens and part-time aliens. This was an era of the convenience democracy. Applying it only when and where it was convenient for the government and the bureaucrats saw fit and other times it wasn't worth the paper it was written on.

From March to June we sat in jail while newspapers called us traitors. The ACLU refused to defend us... saying we had "a strong moral case, but no legal case at all.

JACK TONO SPEECH NORTHWEST COLLEGE. 11/12/87, MIKE MACKEY

Frank Abe identified Jack Tono as " the cocky guy in the high school sweater."

TAK'S JAILHOUSE JOURNAL

May 13, 1944

*Last night Tom Kubo got bit by bed bugs. There sure a lot of
bugs here...What a dump, it's either hot or cold. We still haven't
got our toothbrushes yet.*

May 29, 1944

*Today we had beans. George Shimane found about one dozen
lice on him. Several other fellows started to look for them and
found some. We got some disinfectant and sprayed the whole joint.*

*I didn't find any lice on me yet. We got word from our lawyer and he thinks we have a
good chance of winning this trial.*

TAKASHI HOSHIZAKI, INTERVIEW WITH JFO 11/04/04

GREYBULL STANDARD

On June 12th, the largest mass trial in Wyoming's history began in the U.S. District court in Cheyenne.
It was just a week after the bloody D-Day assault on the beaches of Normandy and stories of the
sacrifices young soldiers were making in the defense of their country were beginning to appear in the
news.

All the newspaper stories about the trial claimed these boys were traitors, cowards, and draft dodgers.
One paper wrote:

> *If these Japs are 'good American citizens,' as some people insist they are, why didn't
> they enlist and show their love and respect for our country?*

The phrase, 'good American citizens,' indeed has a hollow ring when applied to most Japs. Ask the mothers and father of the thousands of REAL American boys who bled and died from gunfire of the Japs.

Let them be jurors when the next group of Japs are granted a hearing for draft violations.

GREYBULL STANDARD, JULY 6, 1944

All 63 Heart Mountain Resisters at trial in Wyoming

The struggle of the draft resisters inside the camp did not go unnoticed by those in surrounding towns. Guy Robertson was plagued by protests from politicians saying that the Nikkei were not welcome in Powell or Cody. Although some families and businesses employed Nikkei from the camps, a vocal minority, including the Mayor of Powell objected to their presence. The locals were petitioning their senators and governors to keep the "Japs" from walking free on their streets while their sons were fighting "Japs" in the Pacific. There was still a failure to understand the difference between Americans of Japanese ancestry and the enemy.

It didn't matter that so many Nisei boys were going off to serve in the army. People in Cody spread lies about the inmates and the resisters. With all the business the camp brought to the towns, you'd think they could have hated the Japanese less. They were good enough to help when the crops needed harvesting; they were welcome to do their stoop labor.

Milward L. Simpson

Milward L. Simpson, a lawyer in Cody, who would one day become Governor of Wyoming and serve in the U.S. Senate, spoke for many of the people of Cody and Powell when he wrote two almost identical letters to Democratic Senator Joseph C. O'Mahoney and Republican Senator E.V. Robertson on April 13th, 1944. His letter expressed the view of a great many of his neighbors...

Dear Joe:

There is a matter of grave concern about which I must write you. It is this Japanese Relocation Center east of Cody. There are approximately 10,000 internees there, as you know. Now the WRA refers to them as "evacuees," but you and I know they are internees. They were driven out of the west coast area and placed in these camps provided for them.

Scarcely a day goes by anymore, but what droves of them refuse to answer the call for induction and have to be arrested. I think the FBI can give you the number here in this camp, and it will run into hundreds. I know that the local jails, city and county, in both Powell and Cody, have been full to overflowing the past few weeks with the arrests made by the FBI. Now, you can appreciate that this leads to a damned dangerous situation that bodes ill for the peace and safety of the people locally.

We have had approximately 150 to 200 soldiers out at Heart Mountain, which has given the people a semblance of security. Altho [sic] they have been inadequately armed, and although they have stringent orders to go easy with the internees, they have been a help. Without notice to either the towns of Powell or Cody, the Army has been withdrawing the troops; at whose request, we do not know. The fact remains, however, that today there are but 20 soldiers at the station, and I understand these are to be withdrawn shortly. This stems with [sic] the silly namby-pamby policy of the WRA to give these people more freedom from restraint. They tell us that these internees will leave camp and go out into useful occupations over the land. If the attitude of the prospective inductees out here is any example of the attitude of the rest, and I am dead sure that it is, then by God, we don't want them away from the enclosure.

It may be amusing to you, but I am in dead earnest when I tell you that I am afraid of what can happen to the people of Powell and Cody if these birds go on a rampage out there. They are a sullen, nasty lot; a good portion of them are not even American born or American citizens. The percentage of native-born citizens who have sworn allegiance to the Emperor of Japan is at least 25% of the total.

I am protesting the removal of the soldiers...Can't you ... bring about some solution that will bring a little more sense of security to our people? I shall appreciate hearing from you. With expression of personal regard, I am

Sincerely yours,

Milward L. Simpson

NANCY MATSUMOTO

Of course, the letter is full of inaccuracies. He writes "hundreds" have refused the draft, in fact 63 Resisters at Heart Mountain were arrested. The total number of Resisters in Heart Mountain never got to 100—no less hundreds! He says a good portion of the prisoners were not American born, but 70% were American-born citizens! He says a good portion are not American citizens – maybe he didn't know that the Issei, like my immigrant grandparents, were not permitted by law to become citizens. He says 25% of native-born citizens have sworn allegiance to the Emperor of Japan. Nonsense. Maybe he didn't know that all the Resisters had signed the loyalty questionnaire positively—with a Yes-Yes to both questions. Native-born citizens, under the age of 18, had no choice but to go along with their parents to Tule Lake. That was the case with my father and his brother, my Uncle Fred, who were segregated at Tule Lake with their older brother, my Uncle George. My Uncle Bill, who had disobeyed his father's wishes and answered "yes-yes" was allowed to leave the prison camp to take what turned out to be a grueling job as a maintenance worker for the Great Northern Railroad in Montana. The plan was that the family would be reunited at Tule Lake when the baby was older, but that never happened. My Uncle Jim (Isao) was born at Manzanar on April 17, 1944.

June 6, 1944. Members of Nancy's father's family who were left behind at Manzanar: Clockwise from left: mother Kura, Bill (Hideo), father Morikichi, Mae (Masako), Grace (Akiko), baby James (Isao). This was on the occasion of Bill leaving Manzanar for Montana. George, my father David, and Fred were in Tule Lake.

YOSH, COLLEGE AGE STUDENT / RESISTER

The stage was pretty well set on the very first day of our trial, when Judge T. Blake Kennedy addressed the 63 of us as "You Jap boys—". We all looked at each other and didn't know whether to laugh or cry. We knew then, that things would not go well for us. Earlier, we had waived our right to a jury trial, reasoning that although we were entitled to a jury of our peers, but our peers and potential jurors were behind barbed wire and in their stead we would most likely be stuck with 12 locals who would view us as the enemy, and would be happy to rid their great State of Wyoming of this scourge the federal government had foisted on them. Much wiser, we thought, to plead our case to a professional; someone experienced in the art of jurisprudence and familiar with the intricacies of constitutional law. To our dismay, we got the honorable Judge T. Blake Kennedy, a self-professed racist.

The prosecutor, Carl Sackett opened the trial saying that he would prove that all 63 of us were "delinquent with their local draft board...through failure to submit to a pre-induction physical."

His goal was to focus on the narrow issues of: Did we, or did we not, knowingly and deliberately, disregard the pre-induction notices for a physical exam? Of course, we did! Why else would we be here?

Sackett riled us even more, claiming that Heart Mountain was not such a bad place; after all, it provided us with free food, housing, and protection. His description of that haven was totally incredible. We had not forgotten the tarpaper barracks, surrounded with barbed wire, guarded by soldiers with machine guns, where we and our families had been incarcerated without being charged with a crime.

YOSH KUROMIYA INTERVIEW WITH JFO 10/21/05

MITS, COLLEGE AGE STUDENT, RESISTER

Mits Koshyama

I remember that as the trial was coming to a close, Sackett was rocking back and forth on two legs of his chair with his hands behind his head. Suddenly, with a loud bang, he disappeared behind the heavy table he was sitting at. Startled, but thankful for the break in the tensions that pervaded the now stuffy courtroom, we all laughed. That is, all but Judge Kennedy who was madly pounding his gavel like a lion tamer who had lost control of his performers. Mr. Sackett reappeared, red-faced over the indignity he had brought upon himself, brushed off his coat, and angrily righted his recalcitrant chair. He then pointed a shaky finger at us and declared, 'You guys won't be laughing when you hear the verdict!' As if he and Judge Kennedy had already conferred on the matter. He was right, of course. We didn't laugh. The circus was over and nobody cheered, as we were quietly led back to our cages.

MITS KOSHYAMA SPEECH PRESENTED AT "JUDGMENTS JUDGED AND WRONGS REMEMBERED," JANM , 11/6/2004

In just 6 days, Judge Kennedy decided the fate of the 63 Heart Mountain Resisters and sentenced them to 3 years in prison. An appeal in August failed. Their conviction was upheld. The court ruled that "two wrongs do not make a right," meaning that "one may not refuse to heed a lawful call of his government merely because in another way it may have injured him." Later 22 more Resisters from Heart Mountain were tried and found guilty. In all 85 men from Heart Mountain were sent to prison.

JACK, COLLEGE AGE STUDENT

One of our friends, a member of our social club, The Shamrocks, was leaving for Chicago, so 15 of the guys went out to say farewell. He passed through the gates and was trudging to the Trailways Bus Station about two hundred yards beyond the fence by the highway. As we looked at the back of his lonely figure, we climbed over the fence to join him and to wait for the bus. Within minutes jeep loads of armed soldiers came roaring up and an ugly situation developed. Being young and hot-headed we cursed out these guards asking why they were guarding American citizens instead of fighting overseas as our friends were doing.

Cooler camp officials prevailed and we went back into camp. Still being angry we wrote a letter to the camp newspaper The Heart Mountain Sentinel asking why we were being asked to serve our country but were denied the right to say farewell to our departing friends who we would not see again for years, if at all. We signed it "angry and disgusted Americans".

A crowd gathered at the bus station waiting for men in military uniforms to depart Heart Mountain.

The editors printed the letter in its next issue saying that it was against their policy to print unsigned letters but made an exception in this case and said that gate passes would be issued in the future so that farewells could be made outside the wire enclosure.

JACK ODA LETTER TO MIKE MACKEY

AS AMERICAN AS APPLE PIE – YELLOWSTONE

PROJECT DIRECTOR ROBERTSON

After all the upset that spring, I felt we had to do something for morale inside the camp, especially for the kids. So, on June 5, 1944 I sent this memo:

Dillon S. Meyer, War Relocation Authority Office, Washington, D.C.

I would very much like to establish a camp for the Boy Scouts and Girl Scouts this summer...I am very anxious to do everything we can for the younger people in the Center inasmuch as they are becoming more and more under the Issei influence. So many of the Nisei have relocated that the school children do not have the advantage of Americans of American culture that they did have previously. Boy Scouts and Girls Scouts and Campfire Girl movements at Heart Mountain have been very active & they are a fine bunch of youngsters. They are not permitted to attend the summer camps of the national organizations and I believe it is up to us to give them everything that we can to continue our Americanization program.

GUY ROBERTSON, PROJECT DIRECTOR, WRA PAPERS

Troop 313's Scoutmaster Hayao Kadota took this photo in Yellowstone Park. Harumi Sakatani, better known as Bacon, is in the front row center, in the white sweater.

An Americanization program! Did they forget these children are Americans? The government put American children inside barbed wire fences, take away their freedom and then plan to talk to them about democracy.

Frank Emi put it perfectly.... "You could say that you are fighting for democracy abroad, but if you lose democracy at home what have you won?"

Frank Emi and his family before he was imprisoned.

Frank Emi had this picture taken with his family during the unsettling days of June 1944, knowing he and the other members of the Fair Play Committee would be next. Soon after the trial of the Heart Mountain Resisters, Frank and the six other leaders of the FPC were tried and convicted of conspiracy to violate the Selective Service Act. Frank was sentenced to four years in a maximum-security federal prison in Leavenworth, Kansas.

SACH, COLLEGE STUDENT

June 6, 1944

Dear Mama and Papa---

Today was D-Day, the day of the big invasion in France. The church bells rang all day long. Some big department stores closed...but my shop stayed open the same as usual. I guess Willie and my friends are there fighting by now. I got a radiogram from a friend who went overseas saying they were well and safe last Saturday. War is awful---why do so many nice, young men have to go out and kill other nice, young men? Whether they are enemies or allies, the boys all have families at home who are waiting for them to come home again. Enemies or allies, there are lots of good boys out there who are going to be killed before this war is over.

Take care of yourselves. Thanks for your letter, Pop.

Love, Sach

HAYAMI FAMILY PAPERS, JANM

NOB, HIGH SCHOOL STUDENT

When I was 13, every morning during homeroom, we recited the Pledge of Allegiance in those days, we saluted the flag with the outstretched right arm. We did this also at all Boy Scout activities. It always bothered me when we came to "liberty and justice for all" because we were in a concentration camp and the paradox was irritating as a pebble in my shoe. At the end of the pledge, I would mumble "liberty and justice for some," fearful that the FBI would make me disappear like so many others, if they found out what I was saying. I felt the same way when we sang the "Star Spangled Banner" the words "land of the free and the home of the brave."

They keep talking about democracy but here we are locked up for the third summer and they want our brothers, cousins, and uncles to go fight while their families are kept in prison camps – guarded by soldiers wearing the same uniform our Nisei soldiers are wearing, fighting for the same flag as the one flying over the prison camp we cannot leave!

Boy Scouts got up extra early to conduct the morning flag raising ceremony at Heart Mountain. Junzo "Jake" Ohara, Eddie Kato, and Tak Motoyasu.

NOBUYUKI SHIMOKOCHI PHONE INTERVIEW AND EMAILS 11/12/04

KAZ, JR. HIGH STUDENT

Our Scout leader told us going to Yellowstone was a gift to all the Scouts who participated in the War Bond and Stamp Drive. Well, we were a competitive bunch.

Our Scout troop wanted to sell more stamps. I remember wearing my scout uniform and knocking on all the doors and some would buy, but most of them didn't and a few of the families got angry. 'We'll never buy these stamps! They threw us in these camps and we're sitting here!'

You know, some Issei thought they were buying postage stamps and when they found out they were defense stamps, they were furious! They thought the Scouts were misleading them!

Most of us Scouts didn't just sell defense stamps, we collected them, too. Just about every kid had a stamp book that we gradually filled with ten or twenty-five cent stamps, one after another. When you had 18 dollars and fifty cents worth of stamps you could turn that in for a United States War bond worth 25 bucks in ten years. Sounded like a fortune to us kids!

Kaz Shiroyama interview with JFO, 11/7/04

by Estelle Ishigo

JOE, HIGH SCHOOL STUDENT

That summer, there were swarms of flies everywhere. That's how the fly-swatting contest came about! Some administrator dreamed up the idea of giving kids a 10-cent defense stamp for every 100 flies we swatted!

Right off, I had a great get rich quick idea. I told my friend Jimmy how we could win lots of stamps. All we had to do was improvise.

Well, we got this screen and made a cylinder. At one end we had an inverted cone with a hole. Now the flies can smell the bait inside the cylinder and they can get in— but they can't get out! The bait — we dug it out of the garbage, whatever attracted flies.

There were flies all over the place, but we went down to the hog farm...there are plenty of flies down there. So, we put the trap near the hog pen and by golly, in no time flat, it filled up with flies. But they're live.

So in the laundry room we...put the trap under hot water...and voila—they're all dead! Then, we put them in a glass jar and took them down to the place where you redeem flies.

Well, we got away with it once— but then the next time, one of them said 'Hey wait a minute! These things aren't swatted! They're not flat. Something's wrong here. These flies are whole!'

They were wise to us and said, 'From here on in all flies have to be smacked.'

So we gave up on that. My inventive get-rich-quick scheme was smashed!

Pigs plus flies and a get rich quick scheme.

JOE TAMURA INTERVIEW
WITH JFO 10/04/05

Joe Tamura, young entrepreneur (row 3, 5th from left).

FLAG DAY 1944

It wasn't just the Boy Scouts who were involved. Girl Scouts sold stamps and collected scrap paper. They were every bit as patriotic as the boys. In fact, on Flag Day Edna Tanaka gave this patriotic speech:

The American flag is the only one I know. On this Flag Day, I repeat that it will be the only flag I will ever know, for as an American citizen I owe it loyalty and I shall honor it.

Scouting was important in all ten of the camps. They marched for every American holiday and other major community events. These girl scouts were marching on Armistice Day 1943 at Gila River Camp in Arizona.

The flag is the symbol of the country that has given me birth, education, and opportunity to live. If those principles have been violated, it is not because the flag is bad. It is not because America is bad. No, it is because the principles on which this country was founded are being forgotten.

Let us, as young citizens of tomorrow, make sure that when we become adult citizens of this country, we will not forget what the flag stands for.

Let us salute our flag and say: As a good American, I shall never forget what you stand for.

HMS, JUNE 19, 1943

BACON, ELEMENTARY SCHOOL STUDENT

We boy scouts went camping at the river and had a lot of good times. But there was one time I will never forget...we saw a patch of watermelons. One boy had a pocketknife, so we plugged melons trying to find some ripe ones. The next day, there was a bulletin put out by the camp newspaper reporting the incident and were we scared.

We had damaged food for our own use. I was really sorry, especially after this notice came out.

BACON SAKATANI INTERVIEW WITH JFO 11/03/04

Watermelon Crop Destroyed by Vandals

Last week-end Heart Mountain vandals destroyed much of expected watermelon crop in our agriculture field. Many large melons which were nearly ripe were cut open and left lay. Perhaps the persons cutting these melons did not realize the seriousness of what they were doing but, if this vandalism is to be continued on other melon crops, there will be no melons for the residents of Heart Mountain.

The internal security section is cooperating with the agriculture section in trying to prevent such vandalism and any other assistance will be appreciated because we wish to harvest these melons and other crops so that all may receive and enjoy the products of our labor.

Agriculture Section

The Heart Mount Sentinel Supplement

PROJECT DIRECTOR ROBERTSON

July 8, 1944: Memorandum to Dillon S. Meyer: Last Saturday afternoon about 30 young boys from 9 to 13 went down by the Hog Project, slipped through the fence, and went swimming in the irrigation ditch...a wide ditch that runs across our property. Where they were swimming...was out of bounds...just across the fence from the boundary line. One of the boys tried to swim the ditch, which was about 50 feet wide at that point.

13-year-old Toru Shibata, was a second-class scout and member of Cobra Patrol of Troop 333.

CHARLES AND ROY, JUNIOR HIGH SCHOOL STUDENTS

I wasn't with him at the time. I remember running alone along the canal looking for him and being frightened by a snake during that frantic run looking for Toru.

CHARLES UYEDA, TROOP 333 BOOK

They started to drain the canal and late in the evening a group of young men got in the water and stretched across the canal bobbing up and down trying to find him. I was standing near a group of older folks who were sending paper boats with candles on board into the water...they were praying to Kamisama, the water goddess. The boats went down the canal and when they reached a certain point in the water, the boats sank. I think three or four boats sank in the same spot. That's where they finally found him. Kinda spooky.

SAGEBRUSH MEMORIES OF HMCLASS OF '49, EDITED BY ROY H. DOI

For days afterwards people cast about for explanations—natural and supernatural. It was said the boy had gone swimming contrary to his mother's orders. His death was seen as punishment for

Bill Shishima recalled that Toru was dared by his brother to swim across a wider portion of the canal. Cold water shocked Toru and carried him away.

disobedience. According to some, the family was living under a special danger this year. It appears that in a man's life age 42 is critical; in a woman's, age 33; and in a boy's, 13. It happened the ages of father, mother and son all coincided with these periods of evil portent...A more pointed observation, made by many, was that if the project swimming pool had been ready for use, as it should have been, the boy would have been there under the protection of life-guards and he would not have drowned.

WEEKLY REPORT 6/30 – 7/6/44, WRA

NOB, HIGH SCHOOL STUDENT

The first group of Scouts went off to Yellowstone on July 8th. There were 100 Scouts from troops 313, 341, and 345. The following Saturday the second group left. Troops 379, 342, 323 and Toru's troop—333.

On "Y Day" 1944, we climbed aboard the back of a truck with our sleeping bags and a few personal items. I think there were about 30 of us crammed in two trucks. We stood up for the whole trip for three hours, but that was no problem.

Our good cheer got a temporary jolt as we rode through the town of Cody where we heard nasty catcalls from the sidewalk— people shouting racial slurs and obscenities.

But, the days that followed were full of happy and exciting moments.

Our camp was in a CCC (Civilian Conservation Corps) cabin along the Nez Perce Creek. I remember the triangular insects--they were swift and nimble. They'd land on your skin, take a painful bite and fly away before you could react— "deer flies!" There were mosquitoes, too...millions of them. We slept under netting to keep from getting devoured. We still had so many welts, our skin had the texture of a giant football.

Their camp was in a Civilian Conservation Corps cabin along the Nez Perce Creek.

Old Faithful, Upper Falls, Lower Falls, Paint Pot, and Morning Glory and all the rest fascinated me. Nowhere else in the world is there an array of geological marvels such as these. There were bears, buffalo, moose, elk and all the other animals that I had never seen before. It may sound unbelievable now, but the Park was deserted. There just weren't very many people visiting during WWII. This trip was far beyond anything that I could have imagined...definitely the biggest event in my life for a long time. I'll always treasure it. I know others share the same feelings! In fact, the trip was such a success that a lot of boys and girls wanted to sign up for Scouts in hope of getting to go to Yellowstone the next year. But there was not to be another trip to Yellowstone.

NOBUYUKI SHIMOKOCHI
PHONE INTERVIEW AND EMAILS
WITH JFO 11/12/04

"We were on these big trucks with all our gear, headed for Yellowstone and we have to go through the city of Cody. And boy, you should have heard some of the racial slurs and obscenities as we drove through Cody." Buddy Takata

SUTTER, HIGH SCHOOL STUDENT

We all knew Yellowstone was famous for bears. At night we heard them scratching and clawing, trying to get into the compartment where food was stored.

But then, one afternoon we didn't just hear them...while we were napping, the warning siren came on and we ran outside while to our amazement a black bear strolled into our barrack! We got out of there. But then we realized Sab, our Scoutmaster, was not with us.

Apparently, he did not hear the sirens and was alone in the barrack with the bear.

Then we all burst out laughing when we saw Sab running out of the barracks in his long johns, clutching his boots, and screaming!

SUTTER KAJITA TELEPHONE INTERVIEW WITH JFO 3/14/05

JAKE, HIGH SCHOOL STUDENT

I was proud to be the designated bugler for Troop 379, so every night, when it was time for lights out, it was my job to play Taps. One night, standing alone under the stars I realized how lucky I was to be in this splendid place. My father was still being held in a federal prison with so many of the Issei. I wondered if he could see the same stars in Montana and when or if he would ever come back to us. I had just begun playing, "Day is done...gone the sun" when I realized something large and dark was crawling out from under the barracks. It was a bear! Horrified, I made a dash for the barracks. There were no more Taps that night!

JUNZO "JAKE" OHARA, PHONE INTERVIEW WITH JFO 5/15/06

Junzo "Jake" Ohara, with his bugle far right, his sister Rei, a pom-pom cheerleader with the Girl Scouts Drill Team and their brother, Tosh.

M.L. Johnson, Wyoming Boy Scout Executive

Better known as "Johnnie," Scout executive of the Central Wyoming council, visited the camp after all the scouts had returned from Yellowstone. He also ridiculed reports that the government was taking Japanese Americans on pleasure trips. He told the *Heart Mountain Sentinel*:

> *After two years of confinement in a relocation center, Japanese American boys and girls are still as American as apple pie...we were anxious to know what effect their two years behind the fence was having on these youngsters...but no one who would be with them would think for a minute they would be anything but true Americans. They laughed at American jokes, and behaved just like any other American youngster would behave.*

Expenses for the trip were covered by the WRA, park officials, and other government agencies. Johnson pointed out that expenses were slight, since the WRA had to feed these youngsters anyway. The only park tours were those for the children, and these were part of the **Americanization** program--which he called "completely successful."

Superintendent Edmund B. Rogers

Rogers became Superintendent of Yellowstone National Park in 1936 and worked with First Lady Eleanor Roosevelt on her programs for the Park Service. In early September, soon after the scouts' visit, he received many letters of protest from people who lived near the park.

Those who arranged the trip to Yellowstone congratulated themselves and their success, but anti-Japanese feelings outside the camp continued to fester. In early September, Superintendent Rogers reported to the Director of the Department of the Interior that there has been "considerable protest over a projected program of killing elk in the park and distributing the meat to the Japanese Relocation Center." There was little criticism over killing the elk; the sore point was that the meat would be distributed to Heart Mountain Relocation Center.

YELLOWSTONE SUPERINTENDENT'S MONTHLY REPORTS SEPTEMBER 1944, HMWF ARCHIVES,

"Americanization" wrought big. Imagine, the irony of teaching American children about the foundations of our democracy while imprisoning them and taking their rights as citizens away. This photo is from Manzanar, but the message was the same in all ten camps.

MORE FAREWELLS

SPEED MOVEMENT OUT OF CENTERS HEART MOUNTAIN SENTINEL MARCH 20, 1943

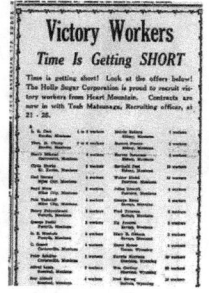

Job listings in the east and midwest were published in the HMS Supplement. Ads that played on patriotism urged those in the camp to do their part and become Victory Workers.

NANCY MATSUMOTO

Stanley Hayami, Class of 1944

Two dozen young men from Heart Mountain, including Stanley Hayami, went to Denver for induction physicals. Now it was just a matter of time before he'd be called to active service. His brother Frank was already in the army and so was his cousin Willy. After graduation Stan, his friends Tadao, Tsuneo, and his kid brother Walt signed on to cut sugar beets in Hardin, Montana.

That summer, farmers were desperate for help.

My Auntie Terry worked at a pea cannery. "The peas had to be canned the day they were picked, so some days were very long, canning until everything was done. It was wartime and there were manpower shortages." She unloaded cans that came to the cannery by rail and were stacked floor to ceiling in the freight train. Her face would be completely black when she finished for the day. Another job she took was working on the tomato line, making ketchup. Her job was to cut out the worms and wormholes as tomatoes came down a conveyor belt. "Sometimes, you'd

miss the worm. At the end of the day, the chemist would check the worm fat levels; it couldn't exceed a certain percentage of worm fat. "I did all kinds of things," she told me.

Young men and women in the camps were happy for a chance to get out of the confines of camp and to earn some money, too. The work turned out to be "quite tough" as Stan put it, but they got used to it. In a letter home Stan wrote on June 3rd:

> *Dear Pa and Ma: All this week we worked very hard. We worked from 5 to 11:30 and from 2 to 7:30. About 11 hours a day or more. I go to bed around 8 or 9. No time to play at all. Each of us earns about $6.50 a day. Tadao and Tsuneo have lost interest in work and want to go home. Me and Walt do not like this work but we want to stay three more weeks. Well, next time I will write more. Love, Stanley*

HAYAMI FAMILY PAPERS, JANM

Stoop labor was backbreaking work and not the way Stan wanted to spend the last days he had before going into the army. So, he was more than "a little happy" when a letter came ordering him to report for induction on Saturday June 17th. Their boss gave them each $75 and sent them back to Heart Mountain. Before leaving for Fort Logan, Stan gave each of his parents $15, which made them very happy and made him doubly so. Induction was a formality. Once again Stan returned to Heart Mountain and waited for another eight weeks to be called up. During that time he spent a lot of time lifting weights, drawing cartoons, and just waiting...

Stanley's Work Card

STAN, HIGH SCHOOL GRAD/DRAFTEE

*Today is a beautiful morning. Up and down our barrack I can hear
kids playing, doors opening and closing. Radio speaking in the
barrack across from me...*

*Well the reason I'm writing again after such a long lapse is because
around next Tuesday I'm going to go to active duty. Probably this
shall be the last time I will write in this book in a long time.*

*Perhaps I should also go over some of the news that has happened
in the last 3 months. Well France has been invaded and the allies are now close
to Paris. Saipan Island in the South Pacific has been taken with the result that
Premier Tojo and his entire staff was forced to quit. Hitler has been almost killed.
In Italy, the Japanese-American are doing a wonderful job. The 100th is the most
decorated outfit in the army. Willie wrote from someplace in Italy. Hasn't seen
action yet... Two of last year's volunteers from our camp have already met their
death.*

*Heart Mt. has been a dead place, a wonderfully live place too. Dust has blown
through it and snow storms too. Someday, from a foreign battlefield I shall
remember it with homesickness. Mother, Father, brothers, sister, friends, mess
hall, movie theatres, ice skating, swimming, school, weightlifting---all shall try to
well up in my throat at once.*

Aloha, Stan

AUG. 20,1944, STANLEY HAYAMI DIARY, JANM

A few days later, on August 24th, the Heart Mountain Sentinel reported that more than 600 Boy
and Girl Scouts in full uniform marched to the train depot to bid farewell to the two persons
most responsible for the growth of these organizations—Mr. and Mrs. Seiichi Nako. He had led
the boy scout movement and the Drum and Bugle Corps and she was the leader of the Girl Scout
movement. This was just one of many farewells for which the scouts played.

JAKE, HIGH SCHOOL STUDENT

Soon after we returned to camp from Yellowstone, the drum and bugle corps played at the almost weekly send-offs. These farewells were becoming a weekly event. There were already 475 men from Heart Mountain in the service. In July, the first 2 Heart Mountain soldiers were killed in action, on the Italian front. Lt. Kei Tanahashi, was killed on July 4th and Corp. Yoshiharu N. Aoyama was wounded on the 6th and died the next day. Both had been members of Troop 379. Another 15-18 Heart Mountain soldiers had been wounded.

On August 22nd, 26 boys, the largest contingent to date left. I carried the flag as my friends Eddie Kato, Tak Motoyasu, and the other boys of the Drum and Bugle Corps marched the recruits down to the gate where buses waited to take them away.

Scouts played farewell music almost weekly.

At least it wasn't cold that day. Gosh, I remember one parade it was so cold and we were getting ready to blow on the bugle and the bugle was frozen, my lips were frozen! The mouthpiece was frozen—everything was frozen. So you quickly learn to keep the mouthpiece in your pocket.

My sister, a pom-pom cheerleader with the Girl Scouts Drill Team led the parade with the baton twirlers and the American flag. It was sad seeing the last embraces as soldiers said their good-byes to families and sweethearts.

"JAKE" JUNZO OHARA, PHONE INTERVIEW, 5/15/06

It really saddens our hearts to see so many of you fine young men depart from amidst us to destinations now unknown. Only old people, women and children will be left behind in this city where once you young people made our life cheerful and hopeful...Your country is calling you. Your country, which is in a struggle the size and intensity of which we have never seen in the history of mankind, is asking your help. Your country is the United States of America and it is your duty to go and help.

KUMEZO HATCHIMONJI HM SENTINEL SEPT 9, 1944 (FATHER OF IKE AND MIKE)

A NISEI WAC

Even as the young men were being drafted, young women in the camps were being encouraged to sign on for the Women's Army Corps, (WACS). In the Pacific Citizen, the JACL newspaper, women were told, "A Nisei WAC will be further testimony to the faith and loyalty of all Japanese Americans." Unlike the male soldiers the women were not drafted, but urged to enlist to show their loyalty to America. Officers who visited the camps assured the young women this was a perfect way to enlarge their horizons, get a better education, and earn more money for their families. In April of 1944 the Mikami family hung a flag with two stars in their window. Their daughter,

Akiko Mikami was the first Nisei woman to be accepted as a WAC from Wyoming. Her brother was already in the infantry. The Arakawa family had four stars in their window. Mary Arakawa left Heat Mountain earlier to work as a nurse's aide in Cheyenne. She had three brothers in the U .S. Army when she left her job to enter basic training in September 1944.

Joining the military was not just a patriotic act; for many it was also a way to break loose from the traditional roles of young women in a Japanese family. Although many parents objected, fearing their daughter's reputation and marital prospects would be damaged forever, those who volunteered rejected the old ways, refusing to live by parental decree. They had greater independence.

Private Frances Fumiko Iritani, the first Nisei woman to join the WACS from a prison camp wrote, "I have volunteered for the Women's Army Corp because I am proud that I am an American citizen. I have a brother fighting with the infantry somewhere in Italy. Both of us feel we are fortunate to have this chance to fight for our country. Being of Japanese parentage in this country had given us both full advantage of American youth. Everything I have, came as a result of being an American. More than anything else, I want the children that I may have to enjoy the privilege of American rights. I want to be assured that when they read in their history books of the attack on Pearl Harbor, they need not be ashamed. They will have the right to be proud of their citizenship."

SERVING OUR COUNTRY. RUTGERS UNIV.PRESS, NEW BRUNSWICK, 2003.

STAN, HIGH SCHOOL GRAD, PRIVATE, U.S. ARMY, 442nd

Oct. 26, 1944

Dear Sach,

The army threw the book at us one day and nite recently. We woke up at 5 as usual and didn't go to sleep 'til 2. That was a 21 hr. day. The army wanted us to simulate that it was a real war and take everything seriously, but the way we took it—we had a hell of a lot of fun.

First we waded through a stream waist deep. Next we had a problem where we "de-booby trapped" a bridge. We crawled under the bridge and neutralized the booby traps (doggone non-coms kept making us jump by lighting fire crackers over our head.) 'Nother time we had to crawl & run 400 yards. And take a enemy position (log cabin) We had to pass through a town and mop up snipers (town had only fronts of buildings Hollywood style). By this time it was well into the afternoon and I was nice and dry so what do they decide to do, but make us crawl along a stream under barbed wire and other obstacles.

Everyone was laughing at me because of the dumb thing I did. (they're still laughing about it). You see, I noticed that every time the guys went through this problem was they got wet all over. This is because when they went under the log they crawled on their stomachs... I had my wallet in my front pocket so I decided I would crawl on my back and keep my pockets dry. So I do it that way—the whole tedious 30 yds. or so. Well after you get down to the end you're supposed to lay on your stomach and start firing at the enemy. So at last, I get down to the other end—I was so glad...I forgot and rolled over into a nice deep wet spot. Laughter! "Splash" I still think it was a lot of fun.

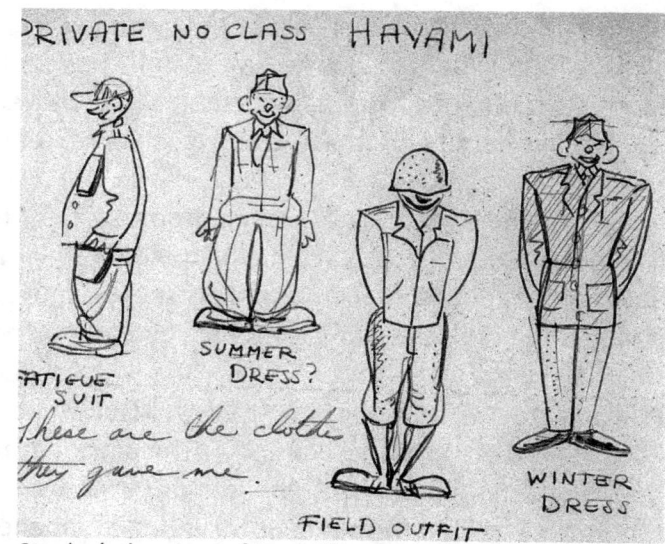
Stanley's drawings of Army life.

Receiving a typhoid shot as drawn by Stanley.

I'm sending a buck along so send me that diary you was telling me about—I don't think I'm allowed to keep a diary but anyway I could draw pictures in it. Well that's about all I guess, I hope you are O.K. and I hope Pa & Ma & Walt and Frank are too.

Stan

SUPERMAN AND OTHER SUPER HEROES

Instead of going out for tricks or treats, this Halloween the scouts went from barrack to barrack collecting their favorite reading material--comic books! Even though a comic book costs only ten or fifteen cents, families living on $14 a month had limited funds for non-necessities. So, the scouts collected their own lending "library" of used comics and circulated their favorites...Popeye, Captain America, Superman, The Green Lantern, and Flash Gordon.

Girl Scouts not only read the same comics, they were thrilled with a brand new female warrior, Wonder Woman, the Amazon Princess, who recently arrived on the scene! Dressed in patriotic red, white, and blue stars and stripes, she's armed with a magic lasso and bracelets that protects her from bullets as she saves her boyfriend Steve Trevor and knocks off some Nazis, while she is at it! Introduced in 1941, she is one of the first truly famous female superheroes, read by both boys and girls.

Kids also read comics in the newspapers. In fact, Superman was a favorite until a series of daily comic strips featured Clark Kent visiting a relocation camp where he was hunting "Jap Saboteurs"! In this series of strips Superman paints a negative image of the Nikkei as traitors who are plotting to escape.

Surprisingly, the anti-Nikkei attacks triggered so many complaints from readers that a special Superman cartoon appeared front page and center with an apology to Japanese Americans in some newspapers around the country. Superman

Nisei Found Loyal, Superman Declares

The concluding episode of the Superman comic strip adventure in relocation camps last week contained a statement of vindication of loyal Japanese-American citizens.

Superman, who had been hunting "Jap Saboteurs" in relocation camps, made this statement:

"It should be remembered that most Japanese-Americans are loyal citizens. Many are

HEART MOUNTAIN SENTINEL, AUGUST 28, 1943

is quoted as saying. "It should be remembered that most Japanese-Americans are loyal citizens. Many are in combat units of our armed forces, and others are working in war factories. According to government statements, not one act of sabotage was perpetrated in Hawaii or territorial U.S. by a Japanese-American." The apology also made page one of the Heart Mountain Sentinel, with the headline, "Nisei Found Loyal, Superman Declares."

TOMMY, JUNIOR HIGH SCHOOL STUDENT

I was one of the few Caucasian kids who lived inside the fence. My dad worked for the WRA, he was the supply officer. He handled the purchasing of all the food and other materials needed for running Heat Mountain. My mom ran the Teletype and switchboard. So I would go over in the evening if she was working that shift and keep her company. If the Teletype was spewing out those messages, I'd glue those tapes to a form that would then become a telegram. I really didn't read those things. My mom said they were private!

Tommy Main, first row, fifth from left.

That winter of 1944 and all though that year and the next, more and more of those dreaded telegrams arrived at Heart Mountain as the Nisei soldiers of the 442nd Regimental Combat Team began serving on the front lines in Europe.

Tommy Main interview with JFO 10/4/05

HEART MOUNTAIN SENTINEL

On November 25th terrible news reached Heart Mountain. The Sentinel headline said it all...

One Killed, Three Wounded in France
'Ted' Fujioka Dies Performing 'Special Mission'

One Heart Mountain youth was reported killed in action in France this week while three others were reported wounded, according to telegrams received here from the War department by "the next of kin...

Pfc. Teruo "Ted" Fujioka, outstanding student of Heart Mountain high school where he was first president of the student body, was killed Nov. 6 while "on a special mission" according to the War department.

The wounded are:

Pfc. Joe M. Arakaki, son of Taro Arakaki, 27-21-E, who was slightly wounded Nov. 2, in France.

Pfc. George Munetoshi Horiuchi, brother of Mrs. Y. Nakamura, 23-6-A, who was wounded Oct. 16. He had previously won the Purple Heart Cross in...

(The following story was written by Pfc. Albert Saijo, who was Pfc. Ted Fujioka's closest high school friend. Private Saijo returned to the center Sunday night on his furlough from Camp Shelby only to learn the next day of the death of his friend. Ed. Note)

By Pfc. Albert Saijo

The War department's telegram to Ted's folks simply said that he had been killed "on a special mission". It was a special mission to make life better, to make people happier.

His friends here, particularly those with whom he attended school, know that Ted's life was entirely a "special mission". It was a special mission to make life better, to make people happier.

That's the kind of pal Ted Fujioka was.

That's why the American flag...

PFC. 'TED' FUJIOKA

ONE KILLED, THREE WOUNDED IN FRANCE,
'TED' FUJIOKA DIES PERFORMING 'SPECIAL MISSION'

One Heart Mountain youth was reported killed in action in France this week while three others were reported wounded, according to telegrams received here from the War department by "the next of kin...Ted Fujioka, son of Mr. and Mrs. Shiro Fujioka, 22-14-CD was 19 on June 1 while fighting in Italy where he was a member of the famous 442nd combat team.

Thanksgiving 1944 was a particularly bleak time, with the flag flying at half-staff. Only a year ago, Ted had been the patriotic one who lead the dedication of this same flagpole that now paid tribute to the Ted and the many Nisei sons who would "Go for Broke" for their country.

Frank Hayami was "home" on furlough when the news came. He and many others who had finished their basic training were allowed one last visit with their families. It was ironic, that he was wearing the same uniform as the guards who stood at the gates of the prison camp where his father, mother and kid brother, Walt were incarcerated. Sach was in New York and Stanley was doing his basic training in Florida.

A story written by Ted's best friend, Albert Saijo, now Pvt. Albert Saijo, tells a lot more about Ted.

> *The war department's telegram to Ted's folks simply said that he had been killed "on a special mission." His friends here, particularly those with whom he attended school, know that Ted's life was entirely a "special mission." It was a special mission to make life better, to make people happier. That's the kind of pal Ted Fujioka was.*
>
> *That's why the American flag flew at half-mast at the high school on Monday and that's also the reason that his friend's hearts were sad. Ted was one soldier who knew*

what he was fighting for-he told me about it. It was after he had graduated and we were both working on the Sentinel.

One day...Ted said he wanted to talk to me about something. It was spring and there was a tinge of color coming into the McColloughs mountains and the shadows were deepening and the evening shadows shifting. We walked slowly toward Heart Mountain, beyond the victory gardens, beyond the cemetery with its scraggly plants and up the hillside. We sat down, picked up pebbles and tossed them at sagebrush, thoughtful. Ted grinned his friendly grin then looked off toward the mountain, becoming serious. Ted could be serious. Ted could be humorous, particularly when he was behind the "mike" and was warming up the student body audience. Basically, though, he was serious. It was Ted who first felt the need of building student morale after the bitterness of evacuation.

He was the heart and soul of the Hi-Y club. That was why he was elected president of the student council and later student body president.

While we sat there, Ted told me about his family and how close they all felt toward each other. He talked about his girl and his hopes and his belief in God.

"I'm joining the army," Ted said suddenly. Though his face was as the enemy's, Ted's heart and soul and brains were American. "I'm joining the army," Ted said, "so that my family will have security. So there will be no stigma against my children. So that I can prove the things I believe in: things like democracy, equality, and tolerance and most of all, peace." Perhaps Ted didn't get to fulfill his "special mission" but he tried so that other Teds might carry on where he left off.

HMS Nov 25, 1944

JOY, COLLEGE STUDENT

Friends at Heart Mountain tell me that it seems the flag is almost permanently at half- mast and in too many windows the flags with blue stars are now replaced with gold—the emblem of those who had made the supreme sacrifice.

When I heard the news about Ted it hit hard. You just never get used to hearing that someone so young and full of life is no more. I wrote to his sister and this is the beautiful letter she wrote back to me...

Dear Joy,

It is difficult to realize that Ted, the boy in whom we held so much hope, is gone; it is difficult until we receive letters from the War Department, his chaplain, and closest buddy—and more recently, when the Christmas packages we sent him came back to us stamped, "Deceased, Return to Sender." When such things come there is no recourse but to accept the bitter and painful truth, however unwillingly. The futility of war is never more keenly felt when those we love are taken away from us. I know better now than I ever did before. Ted died to preserve those ideals he loved and believed in; in a larger sense, he died so that the rest of us could live more securely—in dignity and peace. We owe it to him, and to the thousands of others who have given their all, to carry on from where they left off until victory is won. And it would be so little, so insignificant in comparison. It is a challenge, to say the least—and believe me, we can't let them down.

Most sincerely, Peggy Fujioka

JOY TAKESHITA TERAOKA PAPERS

Just before Christmas a banner headline announced that exclusion was over. Those in the camps had been allowed to leave for the Midwest and East for some time. Now they could return to the West Coast. Ironically, on December 23, 1944, the very same day the announcement was made, 900 residents, the ones who signed "no-no" left Heart Mountain for Tule Lake. Many would soon be shipped to Japan, among them American born children, citizens with no voice to object to their parents' decisions.

The Army Says:

The effect of the public proclamation . . . is to restore to all persons of Japanese ancestry who were excluded under orders of the commanding general, Western Defense Command, and who have not been designated individually for exclusion, or other control, their full rights to enter and remain in the military areas of the Western Defense Command. The people of the states situated within the Western Defense Command are assured that the records of all persons of Japanese ancestry have been carefully examined and only those persons who have been cleared by military authority have been permitted to return. They should be accorded the same treatment and allowed to enjoy the same privileges accorded other law abiding citizens or residents.

Vol. III No. 52 — Heart Mountain, Wyoming — Saturday, December 23, 1944 — 2 Cents Within City 5 cents Elsewhere

Stanley Hayami was on leave when the news broke. The army was in such serious need of new troops, basic training was cut short. Being "home" for his 19th birthday and Christmas was a surprise to all. In a few weeks he'd be on a troop ship sailing to Europe's bloody battlefields. Returning to California was Stan's dream. But his father was not so sure. In all the letters that followed, Stanley asked again and again, when were they going home to California?

GO FOR BROKE!

A squad of Japanese American soldiers are here shown in the action of obeying this command during routine practice on the Camp Shelby drill field. Drafted out of the camps where their families were held as prisoners, they served in the distinguished 442nd Regimental Combat Team. "Go For Broke" was the motto of their segregated Army unit with about 18,000 Japanese Americans from Hawaii and the mainland United States. They became the most decorated unit for its size and length of service, in the entire history of the U.S. Military.

An official photo is labeled: "...night school classes in advanced English are very popular. For the first time, many of the older people are now able to take advantage of the opportunity to read and write the language of their chosen country." Note the poster titled "Democracy at Work" — ironic that the WRA was teaching Americanization classes behind barbed wire, in a prison camp.

WALT, HIGH SCHOOL STUDENT

My Mom and a lot of her friends were taking English classes so they could read their sons' and daughters' letters and so they can write to them in English, too. My brother kept on telling Ma her writing is good! She's a quick learner, I guess.

My friend's brother was already on his way to Europe. He was here on furlough for Thanksgiving. Then, we were pleasantly surprised when my brother Stan got here for Christmas and his 19th birthday. By then, Uncle Sam announced we were free to return to the West Coast! Guess they finally figured out we weren't a threat. They should have known that before we got here!

After the New Year, we were all pretty blue with both my brothers headed for the battlefields of Europe and my sister Sach being a long way from us, working in New York City. The idea of going home to California was exciting. Every letter from Stan asked when we were going. He really wanted to return to California!

But Pop heard things were still rough out there. Some towns were trying to get laws passed to keep any of us from coming back. We saw some of the ugly hate pamphlets that were being sent through the mails. And there were poison pen letters to the editors in newspapers saying that blood would flow if we returned. We heard there were shootings and threats against those who returned early.

Thing is, after the court ruling that California was opened the WRA decided it was time to close the camps—the sooner the better! First they put us in here and then they wanted us to leave! There will be no school in the fall and the camp was to close in November. Pop said he was not going to be rushed. They put us in here and now we will leave when we are damned ready.

Anyway, it took Pop until spring to decide. He finally planned on going home in early May. He had Sach leave NY to get the house in order.

WALT HAYAMI INTERVIEW WITH JFO 11/04/2004

STANLEY HAYAMI

In a letter dated Oct 1,1944 Stanley Hayami sends encouraging words especially to his mother who was new to writing:

Pa and Ma you both write very good letters for Issei. My friends are sure surprised

And again on Oct. 16th:

Well its lights out soon so thanks for the stuff and for the letters Pa, Ma & Walt. Mama I can read your letters...very good--all of the letters were good in fact. Thanks!

And in Stan's last letter before the final battle fought by the 442nd, April 18, 1945

...my morale wasn't too high until yesterday when I got about twenty letters at once--boy did that make me feel good! Letters from Pa, Ma, Walt & Sach and all about my pals! I read them over and over again. Got your picture, Sach. Hope your false teeth are O.K. now Pa. I really like your letter Ma--I understood everything...I sure wish the war blows over quick so I can go home too. Don't worry about me.

Love,

Stanley

TOSHI, HIGH SCHOOL STUDENT

My parents went back to LA in January of 1945 when the war was still raging and prejudice ran high. Our homecoming was not a happy one. A sign, "No Japs wanted here" was posted on the front lawn of our home. My father was 56 years old and had been an insurance agent most of his adult life. Try as he did to find a job, any kind of job, no one would hire him. His license to sell insurance was revoked soon after the War began...The neighborhood grocery store where we had traded for years, would not sell groceries to us...my father was so depressed at not being able to find a job, he took his own life.

TOSHI N. ITO TO MIKE MACKEY

ELLEN, JR. HIGH STUDENT

Pop says we cannot go home to California yet. Maybe after time passes, but not now. Our old neighbor wrote and said it wasn't safe yet. Too many farmers out there lost sons in the war and they still hate anyone that looks like us. So, Pop decided he'd get a job in the east.

ELLEN YUKAWA SPINK
INTERVIEW WITH JFO 03/11/03

PACIFIC CITIZEN

Night-Riding Gunmen Attack Two Homes in Fresno District

Seattle's Mayor Orders Protection For Nisei Group

SEATTLE—Mayor William F. Devin on May 19 directed Police Chief H. D. Kimsey to "pursue vigorously all cases of vandalism at the homes of Japanese Americans."

This action, the mayor said, was prompted by threatening signs painted on the homes of Japanese Americans scheduled to return to Seattle.

CANADIAN NISEI
MILL WORKERS

Evacuee Returnees Narrowly Miss Death in Latest Raids Against Japanese Americans

FRESNO, Calif.—Night-riding terrorists last week attacked two homes of returned evacuees of Japanese ancestry in the Selma district.

The incidents were the 18th and 19th shooting attacks against persons of Japanese ancestry who have reestablished themselves in California.

Undersheriff John Ford of Fresno county disclosed May 22 that the home of Miyoko Masada was fired upon a short time after a similar attack upon the residence of Masaru Miyamoto

RIOTING PREDICTED IN EVENT JAPS RETURN TO CALIFORNIA

LA TIMES, DECEMBER 10, 1943

KAZ, JR. HIGH STUDENT

One day, we were in the mess hall and there was an announcement; that's where they always made announcements, because that's where everybody is together eating. And that day the announcement was about my father! He had been sent from a high

security camp in Bismark, North Dakota to someplace in Louisiana and from there they shipped him over to New Mexico, I think. By then the war was almost over and the block manager asked everyone to listen because— he wanted to introduce my father to everyone!

My father was standing there! And he was treated like a hero! And I was so happy to see him standing there! He looked just like I remembered him, he had not really changed. But, he said he didn't recognize me. I guess in three years I had grown a lot!

Once in a while, he would tell us about the things that had happened while he was being held as a high security risk. Some risk—he was a fisherman, not a spy! He never forgot how when they took them away to that prison in Bismark, when they got off the train there was a circle of machine guns aimed at them. Pop was sure they were going to shoot them on the spot! He figured he'd never see us all again! Heck, whenever he told that story, he said, he was glad to be alive!

KAZ SHIROYAMA

KAZ SHIROYAMA INTERVIEW WITH JFO 11/7/04

Many men considered "high risk" were taken away soon after Pearl Harbor were held for years by the Department of Justice in prisons like this Fort Missoula in Montana and Fort Lincoln in Bismark, North Dakota. They were held without trial and without regard for their constitutional rights.

TADAO, COLLEGE STUDENT

I was drafted a while after my good buddy, Stan. I was going to school in St. Louis when my draft notice came. So, I returned to Heart Mountain, waiting to be called to active duty. Although Stan was not there, I spent time at the Hayamis, who always made me feel at home. As it happens, I was in Heart Mountain when V-E Day came and the war in Europe was over!

I remember Stan's mother telling me—she was greatly relieved because Stanley and Frank were safe.

Then, one afternoon, I was playing basketball by myself when a next-door neighbor told me that there was "something wrong" at the Hayami's.

Stan who was not yet old enough to vote, was old enough to give his life to defend his country. It was a huge price to pay to show his loyalty to a country that still imprisoned his family.

TADAO TAKANO
PHONE INTERVIEW AND E-MAILS
WITH JFO 4/21/05

FRANK, COLLEGE GRAD, U.S. Army, 442nd Regimental Combat Team

My younger brother, Stan, was drafted right out of the Heart Mountain Concentration Camp at the age of 18, and he and I were wounded in the same action in Italy. He died of wounds suffered in battle, dead at the age of 19. I was luckier. My mother received that fateful telegram from the Army informing her of the death of her 19-year old son while still in Heart Mountain Concentration Camp. My mother became a Gold Star mother, not in the comfortable surroundings of her California home, but in the stark harsh concentration camp room set in the Wyoming desert, while still denied the right to American citizenship and access to her home.

There was a Christian church using one of the empty barracks for church service every Sunday. The Reverend Donald Toriumi officiated at the English services and Reverend Unoura presided over the Japanese speaking service...And it was here in the barren barrack church that funeral services were held for my brother Stanley, when my mother was advised that he had been killed in action on April 23, 1945 in Italy fighting with the 442nd Regimental Combat team.

May 7
Italy

Dear Mother:

I am fine and well. We are now resting. The war is over for us for the present. Now we have to salute all officers, keep clean at all times, have our clothe always buttoned, etc. Just like the days back in Shelby.

Thank you for the money. It's going to come in handy. I sent you and Grace four pairs of silk stocking.

My heart goes to you in our great loss. Have faith and courage — for god now has him in tender care. Rest assured that I'm trying to do all that I can over here.

I'll write again later.

your loving son
Frank

His body was buried in a cemetery outside of Bologna, Italy. In late 1949, his body, as well as those of three others, were brought back to the Los Angeles area at which time a full-blown funeral service complete with military personnel with Colonel John Aiso in charge was held at the Los Angeles Union Church.

FRANK HAYAMI TO MIKE MACKEY

YOSH, COLLEGE AGE STUDENT/ RESISTER

After the trial they took us up to a prison, McNeil Island, up on Puget Sound off the state of Washington mainland. We were held in a quarantined section until all the physical exams and everything and we were in what they called the Big House, a high security institution. It was pretty scary in there because there are all kinds of violators—hardened criminals and you're placed in these cages that held about eight. By the time I reached this place, I might have had second thoughts about it—but, of course, it would have been too late. There were 33 in our group and we were scattered all over for a brief period of time. As it turned out, soon after that, we were sent out to the farm, where we could communicate freely. We had open dormitories, minimum security. I don't think the windows even had bars, because--where can you go? Especially if you don't know how to swim?

Originally, we thought we might be paroled after one third of our sentence was served--that would be one year. That's how it usually worked. But, then we discovered we wouldn't even get a hearing! Later on, one of the guys in the warden's office came across a letter from Dillon Meyer asking the Parole boards not to consider a release because we would have to be returned to the camps and he didn't want us. We were nothing but trouble--so he said--just forget the parole!

YOSH KUROMIYA INTERVIEW WITH JFO 10/21/05

WE WERE GOING HOME

Vol. IV, No. 31   Heart Mountain, Wyoming   Saturday, July 28, 1945   2 Cents Within City 5 cents Elsewhere

Center Prepares for Closing Date

By the summer of 1945, Heart Mountain had become what Sach Hayami called a ghost town. Every week more barracks were emptied as families left. The war in Europe was won and although the fight with Japan was not over, plans for closing the camps were underway. This was the headline just ten days before the atomic bomb fell on Hiroshima.

SHIG, JR. HIGH STUDENT

Shigeru Yabu was born in San Francisco and was only 10 when the war began. In Heart Mountain he had a pet magpie, a bird he called Maggie that he wrote a book about years later. In camp, he lived next door to the artist Estelle Ishigo, who was a friend of Shig's mother.

In August, when WWII was over the sirens went off for a long time. This was the first time we ever heard this noise. We did not know why, but we had a feeling the war was over. We laid down on the ground with joy while a small whirlwind stirred above us. We just assumed that the war was over and some of us were rolling on the ground laughing and crying that we were going home again!

SHIGERU YABU INTERVIEW WITH JFO 11/05/04

Hiroshima

By Estelle Ishigo from Lone Heart Mountain.

Though the end of the war was now inevitable, not everyone in the camp responded with Shig's boyhood joy and laughter. Adults in an out of the camp were shocked by the news of the devastating explosion that would soon end the war and change the threat of future wars forever. Ishigo called this picture Hiroshima. It may reflect how people gathered that day at Heart Mountain with the very human need to be with others, to share the shock and uncertainty that shook the world. Inside the barracks there were many who grieved for family and friends in Hiroshima. The war's end was in sight, but what did the future hold?

NOB, HIGH SCHOOL STUDENT

Not everyone was so elated. Sure, there was a sense of thanksgiving that the war was over. But one thing that few people understand is that being freed from the camps was more traumatic than being interned. When we were interned, Dad had a business, we had a home. Those are two essentials of life. But, when we were in camp and they told us to leave—there were no jobs, no place to live, and the country was undergoing something called demobilization. Ten million soldiers were coming home from the service looking for homes, looking for a job and there were probably10 million defense workers who lost their jobs. And then we were given 25 dollars and a free train ticket to anywhere we wanted to go, but we didn't have a place to go! We didn't have a job, no shelter, it was traumatic! And on top of that, the people on the west coast don't want us to return and they let us know with hate crimes!

NOBUYUKI SHIMOKOCHI
PHONE INTERVIEW AND EMAILS WITH JFO 11/12/04.

TEACHER

Sending these families out into the big world was no small matter. We had children who had been born in the camp or were so young when they arrived; they had no memory of the outside. Some had never seen a sidewalk or grass, for that matter. When we told them stories of the Three Bears, we realized we were speaking to children had no notion of what an upstairs or downstairs looked like, no less a house with a kitchen, living room, or bedroom. These were children who had lived all their lives in one room on one floor.

Instead of playing classic games of cops and robbers, house, or tag, they played "night-checker" by imitating the nightly bed checks in the barracks, counting imaginary beds and blankets.

With our older students the WRA wanted us to deliver the message...that they should go out into the world and be as inconspicuous as possible. In fact, the WRA issued a whole list of thou-shalt-nots: they were telling the Nikkei to avoid living in clusters, not to speak Japanese. They were supposed to settle in communities where they could blend in. It was like that old Japanese proverb about not sticking up like a nail or you get hammered! The message was to assimilate—disappear. That was something of a pipedream—easier said than done.

"Some had never seen a sidewalk or grass, for that matter."

Just finding a place to live was near to impossible. I heard from the Yomomoto family they kept reading about apartments in the paper, but when they got to the building the apartment was always rented already or the landlord would tell them right out...we don't rent to Japs!

FINAL EDUCATION REPORT, WRA, PHONE INTERVIEWS WITH ALBERTA KASSING, JEAN MORTON QUINT, AND IRENE RATCLIFFE

PROJECT DIRECTOR ROBERTSON

Just before the war ended, the Powell Chapter of American War Dads, petitioned to get every last one of the Nikkei out of Wyoming. Guy Robertson on August 2, 1945, the camp director was so infuriated, he sent this message to the Governor of Wyoming:

Dear Governor:

> Heart Mountain Center will close November 15th, 1945. A recent Supreme Court decision says we have no authority to detain the evacuees. With the exception of a few...all residents at Heart Mountain are free to go any place in the US they may choose. As far as I know they are peaceful, law-abiding citizens and aliens who are guaranteed protection by the Constitution of the United States.

> I do not know anything about the Powell Chapter of American War Dads.

> I doubt there is anything approximating 1000 War Dads in Powell. Heart Mountain also has its War Dads And War Mothers. Many of their sons are now fighting and dying...for the United States Government. 758 boys from families in Heart Mountain are now fighting in our armed forces all over the world, and I venture to suggest that these boys are just as dear to their War Dads and Mothers as are the boys from Powell or any other community to theirs.

> The 442nd Combat Unit who fought in Italy and France is composed entirely of American boys of Japanese ancestry. They are the most decorated unit in the United States Army. Their casualties were heavy, their record is extraordinarily good and they have the respect and admiration of all Army personnel. They rescued the lost battalion in France and those tough Texas boys were deeply grateful and of course, are protesting vigorously the discrimination now being practiced against the fathers, mothers, brother, sisters, wives and sweethearts of their deliverers. The magazines Yank and Stars and Stripes speak out vigorously in their behalf and intimate that red faced super patriots who persecute their folks might well examine their own patriotism as their actions indicate a support of the things Hitler and Mussolini stood for and against which so many thousands of our boys are fighting and dying.

The petition you received is reported to contain 740 names. It would be interesting to know if people you consider honest, clear thinking and justice loving have signed the petition. I wonder if some fanatical, race baiting, unthinking and unprincipled individual did not instigate the petition and by canvassing the highways and byways of Powell and by cajolery and false information prevailed upon these people to sign something that sober reflection and study might cause them to hang their heads in embarrassment and shame.

Sincerely,

Guy Robertson, Project Director

LESTER HUNT PAPERS, AMERICAN HERITAGE CENTER, UNIV. OF WYOMING

In 1944 Heart Mountaineers dedicated an honor roll to more than 385 young men then serving in the US Army. Eventually, more than 800 names were listed on a new honor roll, including those who served as translators, interpreters, and intelligence service(MIS); staff members like John Nelson, drafted in '44; and over 100 women who joined the WACS and Nursing Corps. 15 men from Heart Mountain were killed in action and 52 were wounded.

The last train for the Bay Area left on November 10. On the morning of that day an organized check was made to see that each family for that area would depart.

> *On Nov. 7, a crew of twenty people made an apartment-to-apartment check to make sure that no one had been overlooked...while we had many pleas to remain beyond November 10, and some who threatened to stay regardless, we had not had any occasion to force departure by physical force. However on November 10, at the last moment there was one single woman who refused to leave and it required that Internal Security physically place her on the train and under watch until the train departed.* (WRA FINAL REPORTS, BANC)

As they were leaving, each adult received $25 and a one-way train ticket to wherever they had a job. That is the same amount that the government gives to criminals after serving a sentence in prison.

LADONNA, POWELL ELEMENTARY SCHOOL STUDENT

On a cold night in November my dad picked up a soldier from the camp. He wasn't supposed to talk about it, but I guess he couldn't resist. He told Dad that the next day the last train would be leaving Heart Mountain. The next morning my dad decided to keep us both out of school, to go witness what he considered an historic event.

It was a miserable November day and the snow was flying and the people walked down over the hill by threes, and there were still guards with guns and bayonets on either side of the entourage as they came down the hill. And it was such a sad sight that I've remembered it. I was eleven; my sister was 9. My sister and I were talking about it not long ago and realized it wasn't the wind that was making us cry. That is my recollection – I've looked for answers ever since....

LaDonna Zall interview with JFO 8/26/04

"The Last of Heart Mountain" by Estelle Ishigo

"We climbed aboard and put our bundles under the seats and up on the racks, and then pressed our faces to the window to see for the last time this camp and "The Mountain." As the train slowly moved away from the rows of barracks, the guard towers and fences lay in the moonlight and Heart Mountain rested in silver light against the dark sky. Slowly they grew smaller as the train crept away through the dark of night.

Our home now was the train as we traveled through cities and towns—still on the horizon, beyond everything we saw, like a mirage "The Mountain" seemed to appear silent and alone-never gone..."

ESTELLE ISHIGO, LONE HEART MOUNTAIN

NANCY MATSUMOTO

My Auntie Terry had left camp early to take an office job in Chicago, rooming with four girlfriends. When they moved to a better apartment, she kept what she called "a crummy eight-dollar-a-month" basement apartment for my grandparents and great-grandmother to live in when they left Heart Mountain in June of 1945. They used their $25 to buy one-way tickets to Chicago. "I remember greeting them at the train station," my Aunt remembered. "It was such a sad sight...they had nothing." No doubt compared to cosmopolitan Chicagoans rushing about in dress clothes, they looked very shabby and bewildered indeed.

My grandmother got a job as the only Japanese seamstress in her garment factory, and my grandfather got a job as a shipping clerk at a book wholesaler known for hiring Japanese immigrants. My mother remembers starting her new school in the fifth grade with a number of other kids like her, prison camp kids who now had yet another adjustment to make. My uncle had left Heart Mountain in early 1943 to take a job in Chicago and by the end of the year was enrolled at Illinois Tech. But his schooling was interrupted a year later when he received his draft notice. After reporting for basic training at Fort Blanding in Florida, he was selected for the Army Specialized Training Program—in which selected inductees would be trained as technical specialists and future officer candidates. He was able to continue his engineering studies after his discharge in 1946 and finally received his electrical engineering degree at Illinois Tech in 1948, seven years after the bombing of Pearl Harbor had interrupted his studies at UCLA.

Nancy's Uncle Tosh.

AMY, ELEMENTARY SCHOOL STUDENT

I remember the hatred in the eyes of the man and woman who ran a restaurant in Butte, Montana. My mother and her friends tried to enter the restaurant during a train stop as we were on the return trip home from camp. The Issei women did not read the "No Japs Allowed" sign in the window. By then I was ten. I could read, and I herded the ladies away from the restaurant.

TESTIMONY OF AMY IWASAKI MASS,
LOS ANGELES, AUGUST 8, 1981

Cartoon by Bill Mauldin

Years later, Norman Mineta recalled that the racism after the war did not fade away. In the 60s, when looking for an apartment,

We'd call up and say, 'Is that apartment still available?' and they'd say, 'Oh yes, come over and see it!' But as soon as we'd walk through the door and say, 'Hi, I just called about the apartment,' the lady would say, 'Oh, I think my husband just rented it and then she'd excuse herself and come back and say, 'Oh, I'm sorry, but my husband just rented it.'…Then, they'd go down the street corner and called the same people and they'd say, 'Yes, yes! It's still available.' So, you know darn well what the mere presence of your face indicated — 'No, we don't want you.' This was going on then, and I think it's still going on today.

HON. NORMAN MINETA, SEC OF TRANSPORTATION ORAL HISTORY

KAZ, HIGH SCHOOL STUDENT

We ended up at Lomita Airstrip…in a trailer camp. Oh, they had some barracks, but mostly we were living in army surplus trailers. It was worse than Heart Mountain. The barracks were like shacks at Santa Anita, with cracks between the floorboards and walls.

And it was incredible. I didn't even want to leave our barracks and go out into the community because of the prejudice. At Narbonne High School there was a Mexican group and they came to our aid—because, of course, the Mexican and the whites never got along. If we'd be walking to school or to the neighborhood theatre or the store, cars would go by and a bunch of kids would be screaming and yelling things at us. Never once did I encounter one of them face to face. They were always throwing something at me and running away. In the school, they didn't overtly express their dislike for us but you sensed it, the body language and the attitude.

They had an office there that attempted to find jobs for the Nikkei who settled there. I went with my dad to work on a farm in Palos Verde picking vegetables.

We had to pick a bushel of beans. Of course, they'd weigh it and make sure there was enough weight there and then they'd give you a ticket. I think the ticket was worth 50 cents and I think I was able to pick maybe four or five bushels a day, at 50 cents a bushel. My father and the other men could pick a few more bushels. That's the kind of work I remember—stoop labor. But that was good for me, because the work was so hard it gave me the incentive to go to school and get out of college because I never wanted to do this again for the rest of my life!

Kaz Shiroyama interview with JFO 11/7/04

by Estelle Ishigo from Lone Heart Mountain.

BILL, HIGH SCHOOL STUDENT

It took about six months for my dad to find a place in West LA, so I went to work on a rabbit farm as a "schoolboy." That meant I had a place to live and food in exchange for my work cleaning the cages and feeding the rabbits before and after school. I didn't see my family much until we all moved back to LA, and even there we had to share a place with another family. My 16-year old brother had a job doing house chores for a well-to-do family. He washed dishes, mowed the lawn, put out the trash and that paid for his room and board.

Later Dad ran a hotel in a slum area. It was anything but grand, but my brother and I had a room of our own and our sisters shared a room. That was a luxury! It took till 1948 before we had what one could call a real home. All through these years I kept moving to different high schools. I ended up in Belmont High with a lot of other Nikkei students and being an athlete helped me make friends. Maybe going to all those schools inspired me to spend my future in the classroom. After college I became an elementary school teacher.

BILL SHISHIMA INTERVIEW WITH JFO 11/05/04

BUDDY, HIGH SCHOOL STUDENT

My parents had a victim's mentality. We were thrown into these camps and so there must have been something that we did wrong. They were so ashamed when they came out. But I said, I'm not going to be a victim. I'm going to be a survivor and a survivor attitude is much different from a victim's.

BUDDY TAKATA INTERVIEW WITH JFO 11/07/04

SACH, COLLEGE STUDENT

In early May, Sach returned to San Gabriel to get the house ready for her parents return. Getting the family that rented the house to leave was not easy. The house needed to be fumigated before the Hayamis could return. Sach was staying at the Pasadena Hostel when the telegram came from Frank. She could not call her parents, there were no phones in the barracks. Instead, she wrote this to them...

May 17, 1945

Dear Folks-

Sure wish I could have been at Heart Mountain for Stan's funeral. I can hardly believe yet that he's gone. In many ways I miss him and yet I'm so used to sharing experiences and beautiful things with him that I continue to do so in my mind and always feel that he is near.

The Hayami Family in 1948; note Stanley is in the picture, too, far right on the piano.

Her letter goes on at length, describing the many things that need fixing in the house that hadn't been repaired in three years. There was a lot to be done, but she adds, "We'll have a pretty nice house. People who have their own house are scarce."

They had rented their nursery to a neighbor who was now running a greatly enlarged nursery business across the road. Still the Hayamis knew they were more fortunate than so many people who did not have a home to go back to. The "glass house" was in good shape and they could restart their business in small steps. Sach wrote that she figured, "maybe it's just as well because we cannot do anything big to start off, anyway. What with Pop the way he is and help hard to get and at high wages. We have to start somewhere and we figure that #625 [their old address] is the most logical place. And if that doesn't work out we can always change."

And that is what they did.

After the war, Frank vowed he'd never return California. He said that if he came home, he'd still be working as a gardener. He married Martha, the girl he fell in love with in New York. That's where he was living and working as an engineer. He did return to visit his parents from time to time. In 1948, the family was together when Stanley was buried in a full military funeral with two other Nisei soldiers of the 442nd.

Sᴀᴄʜ Hᴀʏᴀᴍɪ ʟᴇᴛᴛᴇʀs, 4/10/45; 5/17/1945,
Hᴀʏᴀᴍɪ Fᴀᴍɪʟʏ Pᴀᴘᴇʀs, JANM

Asano Hayami, Stanley's mother and Naoichi Hayami, his father receiving the tri-folded flag at Stanley's military funeral in 1948.

YOSH, COLLEGE AGE STUDENT, RESISTER

Our next opportunity was what they call good time, early release. You get one day deducted for every three days of good behavior…whatever that comes to! Maybe 4 days…but in two years we would be released…some of the guys had extra days because they got into trouble…they were more outspoken. I think there were about 24 of us who were released at the same time. The war was over.

I was released in '46 and it was July 14th—Bastille Day and one of the COs said you are going out on a very auspicious day. I looked at him. I didn't know my history at all. Later on I found out, yes, I was going from an autocracy to a democracy. My dad and my younger sister were there to greet me at the railroad station…the Union Station. It was really something. I had heard about the smog and how you can't see the sky or the mountains. That was something after being on Puget Sound.

Release of the Resisters from McNeil Island Penitentiary , July 14, 1946

On Christmas Eve 1947, we were given a presidential pardon by Harry Truman. That meant we didn't have a criminal record any more..that was good. But it didn't help us in the Nikkei community. We were still shunned.

YOSH KUROMIYA INTERVIEW WITH JFO 10/21/05

TAK, COLLEGE AGE STUDENT, RESISTER

Getting back to the family I slipped right in by going to work. My dad had opened a plant nursery so I helped out that summer till mid-September and then I'd go back to school. I graduated with my BS and started my graduate degree when ooops! I got a draft notice. That's when the Korean War started and more than a few of the resisters went into the service.

Takashi Hoshizaki

Fortunately, I ended up stateside and then I became eligible for the G.I. Bill and I went back to school to get my doctorate. I ended up in the Jet Propulsion Lab and eventually with NASA when they were working on the space probe. My area was trying to grow food and recycling in space or on the moon.

Listen, I was one of the lucky ones! Not all the resisters or Nisei who were in the camps were so lucky. I don't think we'll ever know how just how many couldn't rebuild their lives...the incarceration took away their pasts and their futures. They worked at dead end jobs taking care of their families and giving up their dreams. It should never have happened!

TAKASHI HOSHIZAKI INTERVIEW WITH JFO 11/04/2004

ELLEN, JR. HIGH STUDENT

We got on a train to New York that was full of soldiers coming back from the Pacific. Mama told us not to bother them. She was worried about how we would be treated. But, they were real nice to us. They were so happy to be heading home.

We were so excited to get to New York City! All the tall buildings and the traffic.

The double-decker buses and the crowds crossing at every corner. Our first stop—the tallest building in the world! The Empire State Building! That's where the WRA office is—of all places. Pop took us to the top so we could see the sights! It's really something! You can see for miles up there. I never imagined there could be so many buildings so close to each other! It just went on and on for as far as your eye could see!

Ellen Yukawa, Joanne Oppenheim's classmate in Monticello, New York after the war.

Pop said to take a good look. With all those buildings he was sure he'd find work to do. He didn't know what kind of work he would get or where we would be, but the important thing, he told us, is that we were free again! Anytime we mentioned camp or where we had been...Pop would say, the past is over and gone and we don't need to talk about it. Put it behind you. Now, we will make a new future...a new start!

And that's what we did. We didn't talk about the past. Pop was still angry about where we had been. I think Mama was more ashamed than angry. Even though we had done nothing wrong, there were still people who figured if the government locked us up, we must have done something wrong. We hadn't, of course, but we listened to Pop.

The past is over and gone...now, we must look only to the future.

ELLEN YUKAWA SPINK
INTERVIEW WITH JFO 3/11/03

The Shimokochi Family

Like so many others, the Shimokochi family did not return to California. Nob recalled "We went to a place called Chagrin Falls outside of Cleveland where my parents worked as servants. Things didn't go too well. Then we moved to Royal Oaks, Michigan, where we were embraced by the local church."

NOBUYUKI SHIMOKOCHI INTERVIEW WITH JNO 11/12/04

MAS, HIGH SCHOOL STUDENT

What I remember most was my father, who purchased a Fortune tractor for about $750 a few months prior to the notice. After a lifetime of farming with nothing but a horse, plow, shovel and his bare hands—a dream was coming true. Then came the notice and his prize tractor was sold for a measly $75.

My father was 67 when he was forced to leave his 20 -acre farm. The lawyer who was supposed to lease it never paid the taxes. So we lost the property that he had bought in my name. He was 70 years old when he was allowed to return to California...he had nowhere to go.

My parents had a dream to pave the way for a good life for their children. After the war my mother worked in a fish cannery. She worked until she was in her late 70s to help provide. My father was too old to work.

Perhaps, the thing that affects me the most—I believe my mother and father died very sad and unfulfilled, feeling that their dreams really did not come true. Their chance to succeed had been crushed by unconstitutional and illegal action of the US government. In 1955 my father, feeling he was a failure and a burden on his children died of a broken heart.

TESTIMONY OF MAS FUKAI, LOS ANGELES, AUGUST 4, 1981

ABOUT THE RESISTERS

For decades after the war, there was a bitterness between those whose family members served in the army and the resisters, who were treated as outcasts by the Nikkei community. Their own families may have accepted them back into the fold, but there were some who called them cowards. Exchanges in the Rafu Shimpo newspaper and shouting matches at meetings. It took until 2000 for the Japanese American Citizens League to formally apologize. Even after that there were many who continued to bad-mouth the resisters, who continued to speak out to explain their point of view. They insisted that by refusing to serve, they were defending our Constitution.

And two years later, at a Japanese American Citizen League ceremony honoring the resisters, the Hon. Daniel K. Inouye, United States Senator, a veteran of the 442nd Regiment, and a Medal of Honor recipient, addressed the crowd in a videotaped message.

"Some young men answered the call to military service," Mr. Inouye said, "and they did so with honor and with great courage. Some young men chose to make their point by resisting the government's order to report for the draft. They too were honorable and courageous."

Frank Emi and the resistors continued to speak out in the decades that followed. As more and more Japanese Americans came to understand that there were many kinds of courageous voices that defended America. Frank rejected the mantra that has been passed from one generation to the next: "Shikataganai", it can't be helped. He preferred a new mantra...

NO MORE SHIKATAGANAI!

Hon. Norman Mineta, Sec of Transportation

When all was said and done, the struggle after the war was easier for the young than the old. Our Issei parents were too old to start over again. Most lost all they had struggled to attain, but we Nisei managed to reinvent ourselves. For many years we looked ahead not back. We did not talk of what had happened. It was the past and our parents encouraged us to make a new future and that is what we have done ourselves and our children and grandchildren.

I think the true message of the Japanese American story is that any community can make the American dream theirs, no matter how much others try to deny it to them. But the pain of the internment period wasn't overcome by Japanese Americans alone. It was overcome, and our national honor was reaffirmed by the good work of noble men and women of all walks of life, of all racial backgrounds, who decided that America could be better than it was before. The history of Heart Mountain includes not only regretful actions taken because of fear, but also a story of healing and a proud group of U.S. citizens who found their American dream despite the challenges thrown their way. It teaches us not just that bad things happen, but good people can help heal the wounds that have been inflicted.

HON. NORMAN MINETA, SEC OF TRANSPORTATION DEDICATION OF HEART MOUNTAIN WALKING TOUR, COURTESY HEART MOUNTAIN FOUNDATION

EPILOGUE

It should be remembered that not one Japanese American was ever found guilty of being a spy or for any act of espionage. Remember, too, that over 800 people from Heart Mountain did serve in the military and fifteen of them made the ultimate sacrifice. They gave their lives serving their country. Two soldiers from Heart Mountain were recipients of the Medal of Honor, the highest award our government can give. An estimated 33,000 Japanese Americans served in the United States Army, in one of the most distinguished fighting units, the all Japanese American 100th Infantry Battalion / 442nd Regimental Combat Team. Many others served as translators, interpreters, and interrogators in the Pacific for the Military Intelligence Service. A thousand more served in the 1399th Engineer Construction Battalion. Young Nisei women also served: 300 joined the Women's Army Corps (WACS) and another 350 joined the U.S. Cadet Nurse Corps (CNC) and still others served in the United States Army Nurse Corps (USANC).

Though it took more than four decades, in 1980, Congress established the Commission on Wartime Relocation and Internment of Civilians (CWRIC) to investigate the events that led to the injustices the Nikkei endured. Their study concluded that the incarceration of the Nikkei was caused by wartime hysteria and racism. There was no military necessity for disregarding the civil liberties of the 120,000 men, women, and children. A young Congressman, Norman Mineta, was one of powerful voices that led the way to Redress legislation. Although there was a presidential apology and monetary restitution, the history of this catastrophe must be seen as a warning that we as a people must never allow such an event to happen again.

The story of Heart Mountain is not just a collection of camp memories. It raises issues that still challenge our democracy— issues about racism and defending one's rights and the Constitution. It is not enough to study our past. More importantly, we need to learn from it and take an active role in defending the rights of others as well as our own. This is what citizens of a democracy do in order to make a "more perfect union." Our less than perfect past is not a closed chapter. It is a story that goes beyond flag waving, forcing us to examine the many faces of courage and patriotism.

In all the decades that follow, there will be others who consider their cause good enough to deny individuals or even an entire ethnic group their civil liberties and protection under the law. Right now, thousands of children are living in tent cities, close to the Mexican border. As Pastor Niemoller warned us, who will be next? Today it may be a stranger or your neighbor who is taken away, tomorrow it could be your loved ones or even you. How do we as a proud and free society protect our security without losing the basic principles on which our nation was founded? Each crisis brings choices – do we believe in liberty and justice for all or only for some?

First Lady Eleanor Roosevelt supported the Japanese American community in her radio broadcasts and her popular column My Day. From the start, she recognized the dangers that they faced, and further, how their dangers could undermine our democracy. Her words are as meaningful today as they were in 1941, just days after the war began, when she wrote:

Eleanor Roosevelt

This is, perhaps, the greatest test this country has ever met. Perhaps it is the test which is going to show whether the United States can furnish a pattern for the rest of the world for the future. Our citizens come from all the nations of the world. Some of us have said from time to time, that we were the only proof that different nationalities could live together in peace and understanding, each bringing his own contribution, different though it may be, to the final unity which is the United States... Perhaps, on us today, lies the obligation to prove that such a vision may be a practical possibility.

If we cannot meet the challenge of fairness to our citizens of every nationality, of really believing in the Bill of Rights and making it a reality for all loyal American citizens, regardless of race, creed or color; if we cannot keep in check antisemitism, anti-racial feelings as well as anti-religious feelings, then we shall have removed from the world, the one real hope for the future on which all humanity must now rely.

My Day, December 16,1941 Eleanor Roosevelt

AUTHORS ACKNOWLEDGMENTS

So many generous people have answered our questions, introduced us to friends, sent photographs, and most of all, shared stories that only they could tell. Our hope has been to record their memories so that the events of the incarceration will never be forgotten nor ever repeated.

Nancy wrote: I would like to thank Joanne Oppenheim for having the foresight and perseverance to collect this book's valuable Heart Mountain survivor interviews while it was still possible to do so. My gratitude also goes out to my cousin Laurie Cranmer for helping me find old family photographs, my late Uncle George for being the archivist par excellence, and most of all, to my parents and grandparents for having the strength and fortitude to weather the indignities of wartime incarceration with grace and dignity, for the sake of their children and future generations.

Joanne wrote: My thanks to Nancy Matsumoto for agreeing to work with me on this book and for the time she took to gather family photographs and to interview members of her family. Her voice and theirs are a genuine contribution that add an extra generational dimension to the collection.

These are the names of the many people who generously shared their stories, most were told more than two decades ago when the idea for this book began. It was Joanne's hope to create a "Readers Theater" with a collection of voices that could be used for dramatic readings or productions in classrooms, libraries, or theaters. As we finish the last details, in fact, the book is being workshopped as a play by John B. Benitz, a stage director, filmmaker, and professor at Chapman University. Saying, hearing, or reading these authentic voices will give another dimension and even clearer understanding of what happened to those who lived it.

Although many of those who lent their voices are no longer alive, their stories live on as historic documents—not to be forgotten. It was a privilege to meet and get to know many of them as friends. There were moments in their interviews that brought tears, sighs, and bittersweet memories as well as smiles in recalling childhood pranks with friends and families. For sharing their unforgettable memories thanks for personal interviews in California, at Reunion in Nevada, in Washington, D.C., by phone and emails: Frank Emi, Ike Fujishin, Ike Hatchimonji, Mike Hatchimonji, Walt Hayami, Takashi Hoshizaki, Alice Inami, James Ito, Michiko Ito, Toshiko Ito, Sutter Kajita, Robert Katayama, Reiko Ohara Kasama, Alberta Kassing, Edward Kato, Edward Kimura, Yosh Kuromiya, Tommy Main, Amy Iwasaki Mass, Don Matsuda, Marjorie Matsushita, Hon. Norman Mineta, Sec. of Transportation, Tak Motoyasu, Ray Nosaka, Junzo "Jake" Ohara, Tosh Ohara, Jean Quint, Irene Radcliffe, Nobuyuki Shimokochi, Bill Shishima, Kaz Shiroyama, Tadao Takano, Buddy Takata, Joe Tamura, Joy Teraoka, Shigeru Yabu, Donald Yamamoto, Joe Yokota. And in Wyoming:

Floyd Dolce, Don C. Easton, Louis Kousoulos, Babe Martoglio, Hon. Alan K. Simpson, Peter K. Simpson, Nancy O'Neil Sommers, LaDonna Zall. Special thanks to Bacon Sakatani who has dedicated so much of his time to preserving the history of Heart Mountain. Bacon put Joanne in touch with many of those interviewed, shared his library of photographs, and even made hi-res images of some of the photos. His e-mails kept us from running into dead-ends. We are indebted to him.

Thanks, as always, to the Japanese American National Museum for encouraging and supporting this project. Special thanks to Yoko Nishimura, Project Manager of Discover Nikkei, who read the manuscript and shared her enthusiasm with others at JANM. To Emily Anderson and Jamie Henricks who found hard-to-find images and to John Esaki who gave permission to use some familiar sources, from Joanne's book, Stanley Hayami, Nisei Son. Special thanks to the Hayami family for permission to use their family photos and papers.

This collection could never have happened without an army of generous and knowledgeable librarians and archivists who helped with so many details involved in putting this project together. Our thanks to: Greg Matthews at Washington State University guided us to the many gems in the George and Frank C. Hirahara Photograph Collection of Heart Mountain, Wyoming. Without the Hiraharas' amazing collection, the faces that go with the voices of might have been lost forever. Dana Hoshide, Operations Director at Densho answered questions, led to images. After years of navigating archival sites, seeking images and information for various projects, I am indebted to densho.org for the breadth and depth of their scholarly site. Densho is a treasure.

Thanks to John Waggener, University of Wyoming Archivist and Historian, American Heritage Center, who answered so many questions about rights and permissions and wise suggestions. Thanks to Mike Mackey, author of Heart Mountain, Life in Wyoming's Concentration Camp,and A Matter of Conscience: Essays on the World War II Heart Mountain Draft Resistance Movement, who years ago, generously shared written histories he collected for his own writing. His collection is now at WSU. Most recently Joanne had the good fortune to meet author, filmmaker and historian, Frank Abe on line. His stories and collection of images of the resisters added much to that section of the book.

Thanks to Mack Frost, McCracken Research Library at the Buffalo Bill Center; to Nancy Miller, Northwest College; Calley Steussy at Heart Mountain Foundation; Keri Marken, Center for Oral and Public History, CSU; Molly Haigh, Special Collections, UCLA; Lorna Kirwan, Bancroft Library, UC Berkeley; Erin Hurley, Doe Library, UC Berkeley;Mark Fritch, University of Montana-Missoula; Dianne Fukami, Mineta Legacy Project and to David Mineta. Our thanks to Nancy Roosevelt Ireland for permission to use her grandmother Eleanor Roosevelt's words that close the book with powerful challenge.

Finally, firstly, and as always, Joanne thanks her family for the long hours they too spent on this labor of love. Thanks to Steve who was there recording most of the interviews and there through the final edits, lending assurance along with the time and space spent at the computer. To Anthony who rescued her with all too frequent computer issues with trusty Team Viewer sessions that shortened the miles between his home and hers. To Stephanie and David who both copy-edited the final script; with kudos to Stephanie, who without complaints, added pages of corrections and inserts. To James who pulled it all together, created the cover and designed a beautiful book. It could not have happened without all of my loving family!

Joanne Oppenheim and Nancy Matsumoto

NOTES

PG. 4   "First they came..." Martin Niemoller (1892–1984), German Lutheran pastor. Eerdman.

PG. 13   "In the afternoon..." Stanley Hayami Diary, Dec. 7,1942, Hayami Family Papers, Japanese American National Museum, hereafter JANM.

PG. 14   "Please come home..." Dec. 9, 1941 letter Stanley to Sach, Hayami Family Papers, JANM.

PG. 20   "The FBI picked..." CWRIC Testimony of Amy Iwasaki Mass, Los Angeles, August 6,1981.

PG. 23   "The Japanese Race..." War Department Final Report, Japanese Evacuation from West Coast, 1942, GPO.

PG. 24   "I am for..." Letters to Editor Santa Rosa Press Democrat 1/18/42.

PG. 25   "In April, I..." CWRIC Testimony of Arthur Makoto Tsuneishi, Los Angeles, August 5,1981.

PG. 26   "I was just..." CWRIC Testimony of Robert Moteki, New York, November 23,1981.

PG. 28   "I belonged to..." CWRIC Testimony of Dr. J. Hirabayashi, San Francisco, August 13,1981.

PG. 29   "People in my..." Nels Smith speech, April 7, 1942 at a WRA meeting of governors of ten Western states in Salt Lake City. Smith was not alone in his objections. Only Colorado openly welcomed the Nikkei.

Nels Smith papers, American Heritage Center, Univ. of Wyoming.

PG. 34   "On the last..." Sam Nakagawa, Troop 333 Book, courtesy Kaz Shiroyama.

PG. 38   "I was six..." CWRIC Testimony of Amy Iwasaki Mass, Los Angeles, August 6,1981.

PG. 39   "I shall remember..." Stanley Hayami Diary, May 4,1943, Hayami Family Papers, JANM.

PG. 40   "The clanging of..." CWRIC Testimony of Marjorie Matsushita, Los Angeles, August 5, 1981; "There was I..." Testimony of Akiyo DeLoyd, Los Angeles, August 4, 1981.

PG. 41   "I remember the..." CWRIC Testimony of Amy Iwasaki Mass, Los Angeles, August 6,1981.

PG. 49   "My full name..." Letter from Frank Hayami to Mike Mackey, permission of Mike Mackey to JFO hereafter MM; MM collection now at WSU Archives.

PG. 52   "At the first..." CWRIC Testimony of Toyo Suyemoto Kawakami, Chicago, September 22,1981.

PG. 53   "I remembered feeling..." CWRIC Testimony of Amy Iwasaki Mass, Los Angeles, August 6,1981.

PG. 54   "In spite of..." The Pacemaker, Santa Anita Newspaper, June 14, 1942.

PG. 57   "We don't want..." Sheridan Press, March 18, 1942, Wyoming State Archives.

PG. 63   "Everything is excitement..." John A. Nelson Diary Entry, August 11, 1942, American Heritage Center, Univ. of Wyoming,

PG. 71   "So far, this..." WRA M1.00 Community Analyst report, Asael T. Hansen.

PG. 76   "At noon, the..." John A. Nelson Diary Entry, September 17, 1942, American Heritage Center, Univ. of Wyoming; Nelson Article, HMS, Dec. 12, 1942.

PG. 80   Protest Petition, HM Sentinel, Nov. 21, 1942.

PG. 81   "One day last..." John A. Nelson Diary Entry, Nov.15, 1942, American Heritage Center, Univ. of Wyoming.

PG. 84   Based on Community Analysis Section, WRA, Sept. 1, 1943 and JFO Interviews with school teachers.

PG. 86   Hayami Family Papers, JANM.

PG. 89   "Doggone it! Yesterday..." Stanley Hayami Diary, Dec. 24 and 25, 1942 Hayami Family Papers, JANM.

PG. 91   "Many people have..." Stanley Hayami Diary, June 1943, no day on this entry; Hayami Family Papers, JANM.

PG. 92   "In a temporary..." Seiichi Nako interview, HM Sentinel August, 26, 1944; "Now after the..." 50th Anniversary BSA Troop 379 booklet.

PG. 93   "Find the attitude..." John A. Nelson Diary, Dec. 26, 1942, American Heritage Center, Univ. of Wyoming.

PG. 95   "I wonder how..." Stanley Hayami Diary, Jan. 23, 1943, Hayami Family Papers, JANM.

PG. 95   Questionnaire, WRA.

PG. 98-99   "To the people..." Memo, Guy Robertson, Project Director, WRA Papers, 5/5/44, Bancroft Library, University of California, Berkeley (hereafter BANC).

PG. 100   "Last Tuesday night..." Stanley Hayami Diary, Feb. 12, 1943, Hayami Family Papers, JANM.

PG. 102   A letter by Toyoo Nitake to MM said: "The Nisei had every right to be outraged. Before the war they could join any branch of the service. As of March 31, 1942, the War Department outlawed induction of Nisei, except bilingual Nisei or Kibei to serve in Military Intelligence Service. Now the government did an about face, expecting them to volunteer for a segregated unit Jain WWII, National Park Service..

PG. 103   "Things didn't turn..." John A. Nelson Diary, Feb 14, 1943, American Heritage Center, Univ. of Wyoming

p. 98   John A. Nelson Diary, Jan.17, 1943, American Heritage Center, Univ. of Wyoming

PG. 108   Japs petted and..." Denver Post, April 23, 1943; "Looks like we..." John Nelson Diary entry, Jan. 17, 1943.

PG. 109   "War, by definition..." HM Sentinel, April 24,1943; "It seems that..." Stanley Hayami Diary, April 29, 1943, Hayami Family Papers, JANM.

PG. 110   "We first heard..."HM Sentinel, May 6, 1943; "There can be..."Elmer Davis, Office of War Information, WRA papers, NARA, April 23, 1943.

PG. 111   "Japs in camp..." American Heritage Center, Univ. of Wyoming, C-0151-P9-BU-COS-WP, C-0151-P13-BU-COS-WP.

PG. 112   "Man! It's so..." Stanley Hayami Diary, January 3 and "Today I went..." Jan.

17,1943, Hayami Family Papers, JANM.

PG. 113-114   "Frankly, I believe..."John Nelson Diary, January 17,1943, American Heritage Center, Univ. of Wyoming.

PG. 113-14   Flag Dedication article, Heart Mountain Sentinel, May 15, 1943. Oddly, the article quoted was published in the HMS in May, the real ceremony took place in December 1942. (HMS, Dec. 24, 1942) However, the photo is a re-enactment for Life magazine photographer, Hansel Meith, who visited HM in January. Students saluted with arms extended, the long-accepted way to salute the flag. In 1942, people felt it looked too much like the Nazi's *Sieg Heil* salute. After that, the American salute was changed to placing one's right hand on the heart.

PG. 117   "Last Thursday Frank..." Stanley Hayami Diary entries, August 1-31, 1943; Letter to Sach, September 6, 1943, Hayami Family Papers, JANM.

PG. 119   Fujioka account of Ted's enlistment: Community Analysis Section, Dec. 8 1944, Letter of Condolence document, WRA, NARA, conversation with Mrs. Fujioka when letter was presented.

PG. 121   "I hope you..." Letter Sach to family, Sept.24, 1943, Hayami Family Papers, JANM.

PG. 122-123   "Too bad you..." Letter Stan to Sach, October 22, 1943, Hayami Family Papers, JANM.

PG. 124-125   CWRIC Testimony of Chizuko Omori, Seattle, September 9, 1981.

PG. 130-131   "It's a wonderful..." Letter Ted Fujioka to The Eagle, October 26, 1943, HMH school newspaper.

PG. 133   "I was one..." Letter from Sam Fujishin to MM.

PG. 134-135   "WE, the members..." Fair Play Committee; Bulletin 3, Courtesy of Frank Emi.

PG. 136   "I had three..." Mitsuru "Mits" Koshiyama to MM.

PG.139   "We had bedbugs..." Text of Jack Tono's speech, Courtesy of Mike Mackey.

PG. 140   "Last night Tom..." Tak's jailhouse diary text, Courtesy of Takashi Hoshizaki.

PG. 140-141   "If these Japs..." Greybull Standard, July 6,1944, Nelson, p144-145, American Heritage Center, Univ. of Wyoming, AMC, Univ. of Wyoming.

PG. 142-143   "There is a..." Milward Simpson to Senator Joseph C. O'Mahoney; an almost exact duplicate was sent also sent to Republican Senator E.V. Robertson on April 13th, 1944. Milward Simpson Papers, American Heritage Center, Univ. of Wyoming.

PG. 146   Mits Koshyama speech for "Judgments Judged and Wrongs Remembered," JANM, October, 6, 2004; "Two wrongs don't..." Fuji v. United States, 148 F.2d298,299 (10th Cir. 1945).

PG. 147   Jack Oda to MM.

PG. 148-149   Guy Robertson to Dillon S. Meyer, WRA Director, June 5, 1944, WRA Papers.

PG. 150   Sach Hayami to Family, June 6, 1944, Hayami Family Papers, JANM.

PG. 154   "The American flag..."HM Sentinel, June 19, 1943.

PG. 155   Heart Mountain Supplement, September 14, 1944.

PG. 156-157   "Last Saturday afternoon..." Robertson memo to Dillon S. Meyer; "I wasn't with..." Charles Uyeda, Troop 333 Book; "They started to...Sagebrush Memories, class of "49, edited, Roy H. Doi; "for days afterward..." Weekly report, WRA, June 30-July 6, 1944.

Nisei PG. 160 After two years..." HM Sentinel; Yellowstone Superintendent's monthly reports, September 1944.

PG. 164 "Today is a..." Stanley Hayami Diary, August 20,1944, Hayami Family Papers, JANM.

PG. 167 "I have volunteered..." Brenda Moore's book, *Serving our Country*, p 98. Rutgers Univ. Press, New Brunswick, 2003.

PG. 167-168 "The army threw..." Stanley Hayami to Sach, Oct 26,1944; Hayami Family Papers, JANM.

PG. 171 "One Heart Mountain..."HM Sentinel November 25, 1944.

PG. 171-172 Albert Saijo, a friend of Ted's, who wrote the moving story about Ted, was the editor of the school newspaper, The Eagle. Later in life he became a poet and a well-known member of the Beat Generation.

PG. 178 "Pa and Ma..." Letters Stanley Hayami to family, October 1 and 16, 1944 and April 18,1945 Hayami Family Papers, JANM.

PG. 181-182 Frank Hayami to his Mother; letter to MM. Hayami Family Papers, JANM.

PG. 186 Final Education Report, WRA Papers and interviews with Alberta Fassing, Jean Morton Quint, and Irene Ratcliff, former teachers at Heart Mountain.

PG. 187-188 "Heart Mountain will..." Guy Robertson to Governor, Lester Hunt Papers, American Heritage Center, Univ. of Wyoming.

PG. 189 "On Nov. 7..." WRA Final Reports, BANC.

PG. 192 "I remember the..." CWRIC Testimony of AMY IWASAKI MASS, Los Angeles, August 6,1981.

PG. 193 Hon Norman Mineta, Sec. of Transportation, Oral History, University of California, Fullerton.

PG. 196 "Sure wish I..." Sach to Folks, May 17, 1945. Hayami Family Papers, JANM.

PG. 202 "What I remember..." CWRIC Testimony of MAS FUKAI, Los Angeles, August 4, 1981.

PG. 203 "Some young men..." Speech by Hon. Daniel K. Inouye, US Senator, at a JACL ceremony to honor the resisters.

PG. 204 "When all was..." Speech by Hon. Norman Mineta, Secretary of Transportation, dedication of Heart Mountain Walking Tour, HMWF.

PG. 206 "This is, perhaps..." From Eleanor Roosevelt's syndicated column, *My Day*, December 16, 1941.

ART CREDITS

Great effort has been made to trace and acknowledge owners of copyrighted materials; however, the authors would be pleased to add, correct, and revise any such acknowledgments in future printings.

P.9: Hayami Family Papers, Japanese American National Museum (hereafter JANM)

P.10: George and Frank C. Hirahara Collection, Washington State University

P.11: Courtesy of Frank Abe

P.12: Ibid

P.14: Courtesy of Hayami Family

P.15: George and Frank C. Hirahara Collection, Washington State University

P.18: National Archives and Records Administration Collection (hereafter NARA) (196517.jpg)

P.19: George and Frank C. Hirahara Collection, Washington State University

P.20: USC Digital Library. Japanese American Incarceration Images, 1941-1946 Collection

P.22: Top to bottom: NARA, Local Call Number: WRA no. A-36; Courtesy of the United States Army Center of Military History

P.23: Courtesy of The Museum of the City of San Francisco

P.24: Courtesy Special Collections & Archives, UC San Diego

P.25: Library of Congress: US Signal Corps, (LC-USZ6-1647)

P.26: NARA/Densho

P.28: Library of Congress (LC-USF34-072375-D)

P.29: Courtesy of National Japanese American Historical Society; Smithsonian Collection

P.31: Courtesy of Ike Hatchimonji Collection, Densho

P.32: NARA/Densho, Dorothea Lange Collection

P.33: WRA photographs: Japanese American evacuation and resettlement, (WRA no. G-599) Bancroft Library, University of California, Berkeley.

P.34: Dorothea Lange Collection, NARA/ Densho, (ddr-densho 151-43)

P.35: NARA (536796.jpg)

P.36: Library of Congress, Prints & Photographs Division, Farm Security Administration (LC-USF33- 013297-M1)

P.37: NARA/Densho, Dorothea Lange Collection,(ddr-densho-151-17)

P.38: NARA/Densho, Dorothea Lange Collection (ddr-densho-151-54)

P.39: NARA/Densho, Dorothea Lange Collection (ddr-dencho-151-207)

P.40: NARA/Densho, Dorothea Lange Collection (ddr-densho-151-56)

P.41: NARA (210-G-B389)

P.42: Bancroft Library, UC, Berkeley (WRA no. B-25)

P.43: NARA/Densho, Dorothea Lange Collection (ddr-densho-151-30)

P.45: NARA (NARA-8463829)

P.46: NARA (ddr-densho-37-393)

P.47: Seattle Post-Intelligencer Staff Photographer, Museum of History and Industry

P.48: Top to bottom: Courtesy of Ike Hatchimonji; Estelle Ishigo Collection, UCLA, Library Special Collections, Charles E. Young Research Library

P.49: Courtesy of Hayami Family

P.50: Bancroft Library, UC, Berkeley (WRA no. C-32)

P.51: NARA (210-G-B439)

P.53: NARA/ Dorothea Lange Collection (2001705926)

P.54: Library of Congress, Signal Corps

P.55: George and Frank C. Hirahara Collection, Washington State University

P.56: Courtesy Buffalo Bill Center, Cody, WY, Jack Richards/ Frank Abe/Densho

P.58: Ibid

P.59: NARA (210-G-3B-414)

P.60: Tempo Yearbook, 1944, Hirahara Collection, WSU

P.61: Courtesy of Yosh Kuromiya, photo Stephen Oppenheim

P.62: Bancroft Library, UC, Berkeley (WRA no. G-101)

P.63: Estelle Ishigo, Lone Heart Mountain, 1972, American Heritage, University of Wyoming

P.64: NARA (210-G-E126)

P.65: Courtesy of Babe Martoglio

P.66: Dorothea Lange Collection,NARA/Densho (ddr-demsho-151-49)

P.67: George and Frank C. Hirahara Photograph Collection, Washington State University

P.68: Courtesy Buffalo Bill Center, Cody, WY, Jack Richards Collection

P.69: Courtesy of Nancy Matsumoto

P.70: Densho (ddr-csujad-14-8 (CSUJAD Local ID: HMLSC_TOMO_008, CSUJAD Project ID: csufr_tof_0008)

P.71: Estelle Ishigo, Lone Heart Mountain, 1972, American Heritage, University of Wyoming

P.73: Stanley Hayami Diary, Hayami Family Papers, JANM

P.74: Ibid

P.75: Estelle Ishigo, Lone Heart Mountain, 1972, American Heritage, University of Wyoming

P.76: HM Sentinel, December 12, 1942

P.77: NARA (210-G-E134)

P.78: Estelle Ishigo, Lone Heart Mountain, 1972, American Heritage, University of Wyoming

P.79: Courtesy of Grace Kawakami, Densho, Okumoto Collection (ddr-hmwf-1-68)

P.80: HM Sentinel, November 21, 1942

P.81: Evelyn Dell Collection, Densho

P.82: George and Frank C. Hirahara Photograph Collection, Washington State University

P.83: NARA (210-G-B556)

P.85: NARA (210-G-E99)

P.86: Courtesy of Hayami Family

P.88: CSU Fresno TOMO Foundation, NARA (210-G-E693)

P.89: George and Frank C. Hirahara Photograph Collection, Washington State University

P.90: Ibid

P.92: Courtesy of Grace Kawakami, Okumoto Collection, Densho (ddr-hmwf-1-601)

P.93: NARA, Densho (ddr-densho-37-658)

P.94: Courtesy of Hayami Family, Tempo 1944

P.96: Courtesy of Nancy Matsumoto

P.97: NARA (210-G-E713)

P.98: Frank Abe Collection, Densho

P.99: NARA (210-G-B739)

P.100: HM Sentinel, February 1, 1943

P.101: Top to Bottom: Bancroft Library, UC, Berkeley (WRA no. E-754); Courtesy of Takashi Hoshizaki

P.102: Bancroft Library, UC, Berkeley (WRA no. E-754)

P.103: Courtesy of Nancy Matsumoto

P.104: Courtesy of Joy Taraoka

P.105: Top to Bottom: George and Frank C. Hirahara Photograph Collection, Washington State University; NARA (539726)

P.107: George and Frank C. Hirahara Photograph Collection, Washington State University

P.111: Estelle Ishigo, Lone Heart Mountain, 1972, American Heritage, University of Wyoming

P.112: Top to Bottom: Ibid; Tempo 1944, Hayami Family Papers

P.115: Hansel Meith, Collection Center for Creative Photography© the University of Arizona Foundation

P.116: HM Sentinel

P.118: Courtesy of Nancy Matsumoto

P.120: Top to Bottom: Courtesy of Ike Hatchimonji ; Bancroft Library, UC, Berkeley (WRA no. G-599)

P.121-123: Courtesy of Hayami Family

P.125: George and Frank C. Hirahara Photograph Collection, Washington State University

P.127: Courtesy Buffalo Bill Center, Cody, WY, Jack Richards Collection

P.129: George and Frank C. Hirahara Photograph Collection, Washington State University

P.130: Top to Bottom: Tempo 1944. The 1944 Heart Mountain High School yearbook was dedicated to Ted, who had been the student body president and was a hero to many; Courtesy of Babe Martoglio

P.133: Frank Abe Collection, Densho

P.135: Ibid

P.137: Top to Bottom; Ibid

P.140: Courtesy Takashi Hoshizaki

P.141: Frank Abe Collection, Densho

P.144: Courtesy of Nancy Matsumoto

P.145: Frank Abe Collection, Densho

P.146: Ibid

P.147: George and Frank C. Hirahara Photograph Collection, Washington State University

P.148: Ibid

P.149: Courtesy of Bacon Sakatani

P.150: Frank Abe Collection

P.151: NARA (537165.jpg)

P.152: Estelle Ishigo, Lone Heart Mountain

P.153: Top to Bottom: NARA (210-G-B570); George and Frank C. Hirahara Photograph Collection, Washington State University

P.154: NARA (210-G-G253)

P.156: Top to Bottom: George and Frank C. Hirahara Photograph Collection, Washington State University; NARA (210-G-E926)

P.157: Troop 333 Book, Courtesy Kaz Shiroyama

P.158: Ibid

P.159: Top to Bottom: George and Frank C. Hirahara Photograph Collection, Washington State University; Courtesy of Bacon Sakatani

P.161: CSU Fullerton Center For Oral and Public History (P145)

P.162: Top to Bottom: HM Sentinel, March 20, 1943; Courtesy of Hayami Family; Courtesy of Nancy Matsumoto

P.163: NARA, Work Permit Card from WRA Evacuee Case File

P.164: Courtesy of Hayami Family

P.165: Bancroft Library, UC, Berkeley (WRA no. G-96)

P.166: Top to Bottom: George and Frank C. Hirahara Photograph Collection, Washington State University; California State Library, Sacramento (JC17C:35)

P.168: Courtesy of Hayami Family

P.170: George and Frank C. Hirahara Photograph Collection, Washington State University

P.171: HM Sentinel November 25, 1944

P.173: Bancroft Library, UC, Berkeley (WRA no. G-599)

P.174: Courtesy of Hayami Family

P.175: Bancroft Library, UC, Berkeley (WRA no. H-88)

P.176: NARA (210-G-E591)

P.178: Courtesy of Hayami Family

P.179: Pacific Citizen, p.3, May 26, 1945, Densho

P.180: George and Frank C. Hirahara Photograph Collection, Washington State University

P.181: Courtesy of Hayami Family

P.182: Ethel Ryan Collection, John T. Hinckley Library, Northwest College, Powell, WY

P.184: Estelle Ishigo, Lone Heart Mountain

P.185: George and Frank C. Hirahara Photograph Collection, Washington State University

P.186: Bancroft Library, UC, Berkeley (WRA no. E-723)

P.188: George S. Iwanaga Papers at Special Collections & Archives, The Claremont Colleges Library

P.189: NARA (210-G-K355)

P.190: Courtesy of UCLA, Library Special Collections, Charles E. Young Research Library

P.191: Courtesy of Nancy Matsumoto

P.192: Top to Bottom: Ibid; Copyrights held by and image courtesy of the Pritzker Military Museum & Library

P.194: Estelle Ishigo, Lone Heart Mountain

P.195: George and Frank C. Hirahara Photograph Collection, Washington State University

P.196: Courtesy of Hayami Family

P.197: Ibid

P.198: Frank Abe Collection

P.199: Ibid

P.200: Courtesy of Ellen Yukawa Spink

P.201: Courtesy of Shimokochi Family

P.206: White House Collection/White House Historical Association

Front Cover Photos from left to right: Row 1: Courtesy of Takashi Hoshizaki, NARA, Courtesy of Nancy Matsumoto, Courtesy of Hayami Family; Row 2: Courtesy Hayami Family, Hirahara Collection, WSU; Row 3: Courtesy of Takashi Hoshizaki, Courtesy Nancy Matsumoto, Courtesy Bacon Sakatani, Frank Abe Collection, Densho; Row 4: Frank Abe Collection, Densho, Courtesy Hayami Family, Courtesy Mineta Family, Courtesy Yosh Kuromiya.

Back Cover Photo: George and Frank C. Hirahara Collection, Washington State University

INDEX

Symbols

SELECTED BOOKS BY JOANNE OPPENHEIM

For adults:

Dear Miss Breed, True stories of the Japanese American Incarceration

During World WAR II and a Librarian Who Made a Difference.

Stanley Hayami, Nisei Son

Buy Me! Buy Me!

Choosing Books for Children

For children:

The Knish War on Rivington Street

Bedtime for the Prince

Not Now, Said Cow

Have You Seen Birds?

SELECTED BOOKS BY NANCY MATSUMOTO

Exploring the World of Japanese Craft Sake: Rice, Water, Earth

Displaced: Manzanar 1942-1945: The Incarceration of Japanese Americans

By the Shore of Lake Michigan, English-language translation poetry by Nancy's grandparents, forthcoming UCLA's Asian American Studies Press.

Parent's Guide to Eating Disorders: Supporting Self-Esteem, Healthy Eating, and Positive Body Image at Home.

Contributed to:

The New Traditional: Heritage, Craftmanship, and Local Identity

The Race: Tales in Flight

For more about the authors visit: joanneoppenheim.com and nancymatsumoto.com.

www.ingramcontent.com/pod-product-compliance
Lightning Source LLC
Chambersburg PA
CBHW080839120626
46553CB00009B/2498